NASMYTH, WILSON & Co.

PATRICROFT LOCOMOTIVE BUILDERS

NASMYTH, WILSON & Co.
PATRICROFT LOCOMOTIVE BUILDERS

JOHN CANTRELL

TEMPUS

To George Caloutsis, inspirational teacher, classical musician and great friend.

Frontispiece: Two company employees on an unidentified 4-6-4T engine. Date – probably late 1920s. (SLHL).

First published 2005

Tempus Publishing Limited
The Mill, Brimscombe Port,
Stroud, Gloucestershire, GL5 2QG
www.tempus-publishing.com

British Library Cataloguing in Publication Data.
A catalogue record for this book is available from the British Library.

ISBN 0 7524 3465 9

Typesetting and origination by Tempus Publishing Limited.
Printed in Great Britain.

Contents

Acknowledgements

I would like to thank the following for their help in the preparation of this book: Hugh John Arbuthnott, Tim Ashworth (Local History Librarian, Salford City Council), Michael Bailey, Giles Barnabe, John Bever, Allan Calladine, Sarah Cantrell, Will Collin, Gillian Cookson, Kevin Craven (Research Officer, Lifetimes, Salford City Council), Andrew Cross (Honorary Archivist, Salford City Council), Adam Daber (Archivist, Quarry Bank Mill, Styal), Keith Gamon, Andrew Garnett, Ann Garnett, Emmeline Garnett, Sandra Hayton (Local History Library Assistant, Salford City Council), Richard Hills, Christine Leighton (Archivist, Cheltenham College), Rusty Maclean (Librarian and Archivist, Rugby School), Ian Manson, Laurie Marshall, Keith Moore (Librarian, Institution of Mechanical Engineers), Carol Morgan (Archivist, Institution of Civil Engineers), John Scott Morgan, Tim Procter (Archivist, The National Railway Museum), Julian Rainbow, Ronald Redman, Frances Robertson, Terry Rogers (Honorary Archivist, Marlborough College), Trevor Rowe, Daniel Weinbren and, as always, the staff at Manchester Central Library.

For permission to reproduce photographs I am grateful to the Institution of Civil Engineers, the Institution of Mechanical Engineers, the Midland Railway Centre, Salford City Council, the Scottish National Photography Collection and the Science and Society Picture Library (National Railway Museum collections).

Abbreviations

BL	British Library
EPJ	Eccles & Patricroft Journal
LMA	Locomotive Manufacturers Association
NG & Co	Nasmyths Gaskell & Co
NW	Nasmyth Wilson
PICE	Proceedings of the Institution of Civil Engineers
PIME	Proceedings of the Institution of Mechanical Engineers
SA	Salford Archives
SLHL	Salford Local History Library
TNA	The National Archives
TNS	Transactions of the Newcomen Society

one
Introduction

Wh[W]hen two metre-gauge 2-6-4 tank engines left the premises of Nasmyth, Wilson & Co. Ltd. destined for service on the South Indian Railway in 1938,[1] a century of locomotive manufacture at the Bridgewater Foundry, Patricroft, came to an end. The company had become the latest victim of an industry-wide rationalization programme that had already brought about a number of amalgamations and closures so reducing the number of active builders from fourteen to ten.[2] Although Nasmyth Wilson was one of the longest surviving locomotive-builders – only three firms had a longer trading history by 1938[3] – it had never achieved the production capacity of its North West neighbours, The Vulcan Foundry of Newton-le-Willows and Beyer Peacock & Co. of Gorton, Manchester. Nasmyth Wilson was, in fact, the smallest of the major locomotive builders with a total output of just 1,632 engines.[4] Yet the qualities of its products were much admired. In 1913, *The Railway Gazette* claimed that the firm was 'renowned throughout the world' and that there were few countries 'where the pyramid shaped name plate... is not well known and respected as a hall-mark of excellent workmanship'.[5] In 1939 the same journal stated that the name of Nasmyth Wilson had 'always been an honoured one in the locomotive industry', an industry that enjoyed an international reputation for its 'soundness of design, excellence of workmanship, and reliability in service.'[6]

Nasmyth Wilson's survival as a locomotive builder into the twentieth century owed much to the fact that it never depended entirely upon locomotive manufacture for its business. In one hundred years of locomotive production no engines were produced in twenty of those years, especially between the mid 1850s and early 1870s. In those years of locomotive famine, the firm was able to survive on sales of steam hammers, hydraulic cotton presses, machine tools, steam engines and other miscellaneous engineering and foundry products, many of which were protected by patent. This diversity reflected the inventive skills of the two engineers remembered in the name of the firm, James Nasmyth (1808-1890), the principal founder, and Robert Wilson (1803-1882). It was James Nasmyth, in particular, whose name and reputation lent a definite kudos to the firm and ensured that its locomotives were regarded with more than ordinary respect. Apart from George and Robert Stephenson, Nasmyth was the only locomotive manufacturer to attract the serious literary attentions of Samuel Smiles who included him amongst his subjects for *Industrial Biography* published in 1863[7] and, twenty years later, edited his *Autobiography*.[8] These works helped establish James Nasmyth in the public eye as one of the great engineers of the Victorian Age. Robert Wilson always lived in the shadow of his more famous associate yet played a pivotal role in the success of the firm both during the Nasmyth years and after the latter's early retirement at the end of 1856.

Nasmyth Wilson did not become the name of the business operating from the Bridgewater Foundry until 1867. The firm was established on its Patricroft site in 1836 following the decision of the partnership of J&G Nasmyth to move out of its Manchester-based workshop to a green field site some six miles to the west. Between 1836 and 1867 the firm was variously known as Nasmyths Gaskell & Co. (1836-1842), Nasmyth Gaskell & Co. (1842-1850) and James Nasmyth & Co. (1850-1867).

In 1882 the firm became a limited company, Nasmyth, Wilson & Co. Ltd. Following the Companies Act of 1907, which provided a legal distinction between public and private companies, Nasmyth Wilson converted into a private company in June 1908. In August 1919 it reconverted to a public company retaining this status until voting to go into voluntary liquidation in November 1940. The change from partnership to limited company did not essentially change the nature of the firm until after the First World War. Prior to that share ownership was restricted to directors, senior employees and those with obvious connections with the firm. After 1919 control passed into the hands of a Sheffield steel-making company.

When Nasmyths Gaskell accepted its first order for locomotive manufacture from the London & Southampton Railway in 1838 the locomotive-building industry was undergoing a rapid expansion following the success of the Liverpool-Manchester Railway and the formation of new railway companies. Estimated annual production by the leading manufacturers had increased from twenty locomotives in 1831 to 171 in 1838. In the North West, which was displacing the North East as the main centre of the industry, the most important firms were Edward Bury of Liverpool, Rothwell, Hick & Rothwell of Bolton, Charles Tayleur & Co. (later The Vulcan Foundry Co.) and Jones, Turner & Evans of Newton-le-Willows, the Haigh Foundry of Wigan and Sharp Roberts of Manchester. William Fairbairn of Manchester began locomotive production at the same time as Nasmyths Gaskell. All these early locomotive-building firms were established as general engineers, often with connections to specific types of engineering product such as textile machinery – Sharp Roberts – or winding engines and pumping equipment for the mining industry – the Haigh Foundry. By 1865 all had ceased trading with the exception of The Vulcan Foundry, Sharp Stewart (formerly Sharp Roberts) and what was to become Nasmyth Wilson. Part of the problem was that from the early 1840s the private locomotive manufacturers were increasingly denied access to the home market as the larger railway companies decided to design and produce their rolling stock in-house. The Crewe works of the Grand Junction Railway produced its first locomotive in 1843, followed by the Swindon works

NW 1650 of 1938 for South Indian Railway with Albert Platts, foreman of the erecting shed. The last locomotive built by Nasmyth, Wilson & Co. Ltd. (SLHL)

NW 1650 of 1938 at Maguram, 1977. (Bawcutt Collection, National Railway Museum)

Below and next page: *Engineering products manufactured at the Bridgewater Foundry*

Above left: *James Nasmyth with one of the company's steam hammers, 1855. (SLHL)*
Above right: *Vertical hydraulic three-cylinder packing press, patented 1862. (SLHL)*

Above: *Punching and shearing machine, 1862. (SLHL)*

Below: *Horizontal pumping engine, 1876. (SLHL)*

of the Great Western and the Miles Platting works of the Manchester & Leeds Railway in 1846. During the 1840s, fourteen per cent of main line domestic demand was met by the railway company workshops and this rose to forty-one per cent and fifty-three per cent during the two succeeding decades. The private locomotive-building firms were able to pick up domestic orders from the major railway companies in years of excess demand and were always able to supply the smaller railways and industrial undertakings but, for the most part, they had to look abroad for the bulk of their business. This was a handicap unique to the British private manufacturers, for their main competitors enjoyed extensive access to their home markets and in Germany all the steam locomotives were built by private industry.

Locomotive production at the Bridgewater Foundry reflected these market trends. Between 1838 and 1853, when James Nasmyth was the managing partner, fewer than four per cent of locomotives manufactured were sent abroad. During the Wilson years, 1857 to 1882, this had risen to eighty per cent and rose again to ninety-two per cent in the period 1882 to 1914. During the 1930s all the locomotives produced were for the export market. Of the total of 1,632 locomotives manufactured at Patricroft, 372 engines, or twenty-three per cent, were produced for the home market, including Ireland, and this total included 100 Class 0-4-0 petrol–electric engines produced for the Ministry of Munitions during the First World War. The principal overseas destinations were India and Burma which accounted for forty-eight per cent of exports followed by Japan, fifteen per cent, and Africa, eleven per cent. This export dependence ultimately led to the demise of the firm especially since the locomotive trade became increasingly important within the engineering activities of the Bridgewater Foundry. Although locomotive manufacture lasted throughout a hundred years, 1,279 engines, or seventy-eight per cent of the total, were built during the second half of the century. It was almost certainly during the 1880s that locomotive building became the principal part of the business

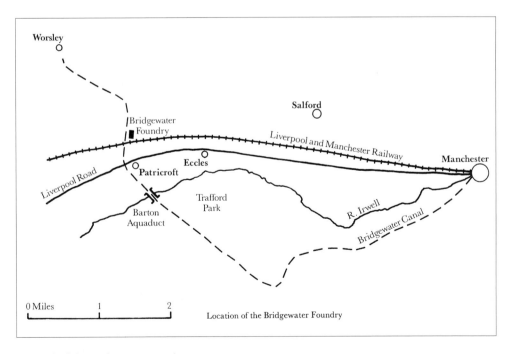

Location of the Bridgewater Foundry.

Above and below: *Two phases in the life of a Nasmyth locomotive (NW 454 of 1894): 1. At Brown Bayley's Steel Co. Sheffield. (SLHL) 2. Posing as* Oswald the Talking Engine *at the Midland Railway Centre, 2003. (Midland Railway Centre)*

and an account of 1887 claimed that the Bridgewater Foundry had the capacity to produce one locomotive per week.[9]

Amongst the leading locomotive builders Nasmyth Wilson is one of the last to attract the attentions of the historian.[10] Yet quite apart from a number of preserved locomotives[11] there is a substantial archive of the firm's business records with the survival of sources relating to locomotive specification, accounts, orders, sales and correspondence.[12] At the very least these facilitate the compilation of a comprehensive listing of locomotives manufactured at the Bridgewater Foundry together with some basic market analysis. But they also enable a considerable amount of detail to be added in terms of the establishment and capitalisation of the business, the organization and layout of the factory, the quality of management, the nature of the workforce, the combining of locomotive manufacture with general engineering and some of the problems encountered with regard to pricing and competition. It is the purpose of this short study to investigate the origins of the firm and its entry into the locomotive trade, the progress towards an export-led business which blossomed during the Edwardian Age, and the dramatic fall in orders following the world recession of the 1930s.

two
Foundations

The early years of the Bridgewater Foundry rested on three elements: the engineering talents of George and James Nasmyth, the business acumen of Holbrook Gaskell and the financial backing of Birley & Co., soon to be replaced by Henry Garnett and George Humphrys. Robert Wilson was not involved with the establishment of the firm though he joined the Nasmyths as works manager in 1840.

Unlike many of their engineering contemporaries – such as Richard Roberts, William Fairbairn or Robert Wilson – the Nasmyth brothers had enjoyed every advantage of upbringing, education and training. George[1] and James Nasmyth[2] were the third and fourth sons of Alexander Nasmyth (1758-1840)[3] and Barbara Foulis (1765-1848). George was born in 1806 and James two years later by which time their father was in his fifty-first year.[4] Alexander Nasmyth was a celebrated landscape and portrait painter while his wife, Barbara, although without a fortune, was the sister of the baronet Sir James Foulis. The family lived a comfortable existence in a two-storey apartment at the top of a substantial house in York Place, Edinburgh. The household supported a nursemaid and servants and Alexander's friends and acquaintances included some of the most eminent scientists, artists and literary men in Scotland – James Nasmyth recalls the visits of Sir Walter Scott, James Watt and Sir Henry Raeburn.

The Nasmyth brothers received their first instruction in mechanics from Alexander who maintained an attic workshop equipped with a small furnace stove, an anvil, tongs, foot lathe and bench. He was also able to offer his sons lessons in draughtsmanship. Formal schooling was less satisfactory and James' interest in classical learning was extinguished by the harsh discipline of his teachers, the traditional methods of 'rote and cram' and the classes of nearly 200 boys. George and James left the Edinburgh High School in the early 1820s. For the next seven or eight years they pursued their interests in mechanics at home and in the company of friends while receiving theoretical instruction at the Edinburgh School of Arts, the forerunner of Heriot-Watt University, and at Edinburgh University where they attended lectures in chemistry, geometry, mathematics and natural philosophy. Their home-based manufacturing activities included the production of spinning tops, small brass cannon and model steam engines.

The most ambitious engineering project undertaken by the Nasmyth brothers during these formative years was a road steam carriage. This was their first venture into the world of locomotion. The records of the Edinburgh Society of Arts show that this machine was originally designed to carry six persons,[5] though James Nasmyth's later description and illustration refer to a carriage which could accommodate eight passengers and two operators. It apparently made a number of successful trials on the Queensferry Road near Edinburgh. Shortly after this the Nasmyth brothers accompanied their father to London where they were able to persuade the most renowned mechanical engineer of the city, Henry Maudslay, to appoint them as his personal assistants. The Nasmyths remained with Maudslay from May 1829 until six months after the latter's death in February 1831. Prior to this, in September 1830, James Nasmyth, almost certainly accompanied by his brother, attended the opening of the Liverpool & Manchester Railway. While watching this event the younger brother produced a sketch of what he thought was the *Rocket*.[6]

After leaving the Lambeth Works of Maudslay Sons & Field in August 1831 the Nasmyth brothers returned to Edinburgh where they spent the next three years engaged in workshop engineering activities while preparing a set of tools and other equipment in readiness for setting up independent business. By 1834 they had accumulated £63 capital and decided to seek their fortune in Manchester, a town that was already the engineering capital of the north where the rents and wage rates were substantially below those of London. The Nasmyths entered into an agreement with Wren & Bennett, agents for Boulton & Watt, for the lease of a factory flat forming the first floor of a disused cotton mill in Dale Street, off Piccadilly. At this stage the firm traded as J&G Nasmyth.[7] There were no sleeping partners though there were offers of credit facilities amounting to £1,500 from two local businessmen. Orders poured in and the Nasmyths were soon fully engaged producing small steam engines, parts for printing machines and flat surfaces with their planing machine. The premises allowed little scope for expansion, however, and as the business prospered the partners felt the need to escape from the confinement of a small workshop. Matters were brought to a head when the beam of a 20hp engine crashed through the workshop floor on to the premises of a glass cutter located below.

James Nasmyth claimed that he had first appreciated the advantages of the Patricroft site while en route to Liverpool in September 1830. The transport advantages were obvious for the area lay close to the intersection of the Bridgewater Canal and Liverpool & Manchester Railway, so providing convenient access to every port and industrial region in the country. A surviving schedule of deeds dated 1930 indicates that on 31 December 1835 the Nasmyths leased a plot of land covering an area of 13,536 square yards from Thomas Joseph Trafford Esq. on the western side of Green Lane, Patricroft, and that in May and October 1836 adjoining plots of land covering areas of 5,030 square yards and 46,463 square yards respectively were leased from George Cornwall Legh on the eastern side of Green Lane.[8] The October leasing agreement was also signed by Holbrook Gaskell and marks the beginning of his fourteen year association with the firm.

Holbrook Gaskell was James Nasmyth's longest serving and best known working partner.[9] He was born in 1813 at Wavertree, Lancashire, the eldest son of cousins, Roger Gaskell and Ann Hunter. Based in Liverpool, his father managed the commercial offshoot of a Warrington sailcloth firm, a business in which the Gaskell family had been prominent traders and manufacturers during the eighteenth century. Gaskell began his education at a private school in Norton, near Sheffield, run by a Unitarian minister. At the age of fourteen, he became apprenticed to Yates & Cox, Liverpool iron merchants and nail makers, where his duties were mainly clerical. On attaining his majority, Gaskell began looking for alternative openings since there was little prospect of obtaining a partnership with his employers. He considered reading for the Bar and a more adventurous scheme of settling in the East Indies. While still undecided about his future he was introduced to the Nasmyths by Thomas Jevons, a Liverpool iron merchant and nail maker. With the expansion of their business the Nasmyth brothers were looking for someone to attend to 'the counting-house, the correspondence and the arrangement of money affairs'. Gaskell came to his new post with the benefit of nine years' commercial experience and left behind him a high reputation. His employer R.V. Yates, wrote in December 1834, that his conduct had been 'perfectly excellent and praiseworthy'.

Gaskell injected a 'moderate amount of capital' into the partnership which, by June 1838, amounted to £4,859, almost twice the combined capital of the Nasmyth brothers at that date. His main responsibility at the Bridgewater Foundry was the control of commercial operations. This involved supervising the pay-roll, obtaining the best deals with bankers, merchants, and suppliers, keeping a steady check on customer accounts, making discreet enquiries regarding credit status and all the thousand and one tasks involved in running the financial side of a

Left: *James Nasmyth by D.O. Hill, c.1845. (Scottish National Photography Collection)*

Below: *The Nasmyth brothers' road steam carriage. (Smiles, 1883)*

business. It would appear that Gaskell's abilities in this area were out of the ordinary for his success with Nasmyth was later repeated in a partnership with Henry Deacon: during the 1860s Gaskell Deacon & Co. became one of the largest and most profitable Leblanc manufacturies in Widnes.

Gaskell's contribution to the Bridgewater Foundry was to keep it on a sound financial basis especially during the early years. This must have brought him into conflict with James Nasmyth who noted in his *Autobiography* that Gaskell refused to provide the funds for the patenting of his steam hammer. An undated letter to Gaskell from his brother, Hunter, refers to a 'flare up with J.N.' and in reference to Nasmyth stated that it 'must be a most unpleasant task to work with a man in whom you have no confidence'.[10] The cause of this disagreement remains unclear but appears to relate to the allocation of money resulting from Nasmyth's patented inventions. Shortly after Gaskell's retirement in 1850 Nasmyth referred to his 'late troublesome small-minded partner' in a letter to Charles Babbage.[11] The reason for Gaskell's withdrawal from the partnership was a head injury sustained in the foundry. The fourteen-year association between Gaskell and the Bridgewater Foundry was an undoubted business success and although Nasmyth and Gaskell may have disliked one another, the latter's calm, methodical thoroughness was the ideal counterpoint to his partner's more volatile and inspirational nature. By the time Nasmyth wrote his *Autobiography* he was able to refer to his 'worthy partner', noted his 'frank and friendly manner' and the 'hearty zeal' of their working relationship. Gaskell was the bedrock of the early years of the business.

The principal financial risk with regard to the Bridgewater Foundry was taken by Birley & Co., Manchester cotton manufacturers. The senior representatives of this firm were Hugh Hornby Birley (1778-1845), who had been a member of the Provisional Committee of the Liverpool & Manchester Railway in 1822, and his younger brother, Joseph (1782-1847), whose sons, Thomas Hornby and Richard, also signed the 1836 partnership agreement. H.H. and Joseph Birley were the grandsons of John Birley of Kirkham (d.1767), who was originally a West Indian merchant in the firm of Birley & Alker, but later made the transition to flax manufacturing. John's second son, Richard (1743-1813), moved to Blackburn where he continued the manufacturing tradition, this time in cotton, with Richard Cardwell and John Hornby. Richard's second and third sons, H.H. and Joseph Birley, migrated further south to Manchester where they joined forces with Peter Marsland in 1802 at Chorlton Mills.[12] By the 1830s their business was one of the largest in the Manchester area.

The Birleys were interested in inventors and men with innovatory ideas and in 1824 they entered partnership with Charles Macintosh who had recently patented his process for manufacturing waterproof cloth. By 1836, they also had substantial investments in the Hartlepool Dock & Railway Company and the Macclesfield Canal. It was therefore quite in character with their catholic business tastes that they should become interested in two talented and well trained engineers. The Birleys may also been looking for a trustworthy source of engineering products for their various business ventures. It appears that they acted with caution – both the Nasmyth brothers and Gaskell were young and with no experience of managing a large-scale business. Hence, according to legend, the Bridgewater Foundry was so designed as to permit conversion to cotton spinning. The five-storey building at the southern end of the factory fulfilled this requirement and became known as the 'mill building';[13] with the exception of light machine work, pattern making and storage, the four flats were obviously unsuitable for most work connected with engineering.

By the end of March 1837, the Birley capital amounted to £4,883 and this was increased by financial injections of £12,201, £13,710 and £8,855 during the following eighteen months. The final balance of £41,139 constituted eighty-seven per cent of the investments placed in

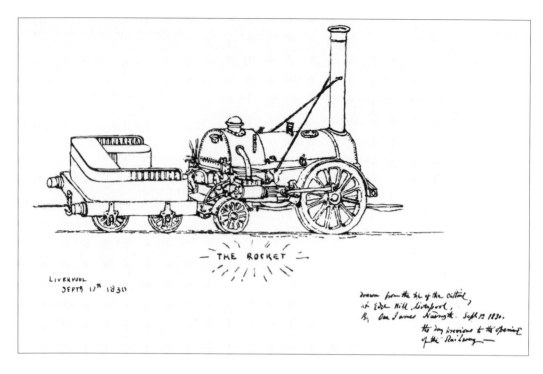

Nasmyth's sketch of the Northumbrian *mistaken for the* Rocket *in September 1830. (SLHL)*

the new enterprise. But the Birley investment was to be short lived and they withdrew from the partnership on 30 June 1838 after approximately two years making their final financial withdrawal in March 1839. They transferred their investment to John George Bodmer, another highly talented engineer but with a decided interest in cotton spinning and preparation.

Nasmyth's new financial backers were George Humphrys and Henry Garnett, who contributed their capital in equal proportions and probably invested about £20,000 each. The new investment was considerably safer than that originally placed by the Birleys, for the factory was now complete and beginning to prosper with a rapidly expanding sales base. George Humphrys had been introduced to the Nasmyths by Edward Loyd – he was the latter's solicitor. Humphrys had been acting as the Nasmyths' legal advisor since 1835 and had therefore been in a favourable position to judge the investment potential of the new concern. His motives for investment were most likely confined to the expectation of a good financial return. Humphrys moved to London in 1843 and withdrew from Nasmyth Gaskell & Co. in June 1848.

Henry Garnett's entry to the firm in June 1838 began an association between the Garnett family and the Bridgewater Foundry that was to extend into the twentieth century.[14] Henry's grandfather, John Garnett (1743-1800), became a mercantile trader with Jamaican connections based in Ulverston. In 1794 he moved to Manchester where he practised as a cotton and twist dealer. After his death, the Manchester activities were continued by his third and fourth sons, Robert (1780-1852) and William (1782-1863). Henry Garnett, the third son of Robert Garnett, was born in 1814. By 1838 he would have been just twenty-four years old and the Nasmyth investment, although nominally from him, must have come from his father. It is highly probable that Nasmyths Gaskell & Co. were introduced to the Garnetts by one of the Birleys. Leading Manchester cotton merchants and manufacturers were certain to know each other and

William Garnett's name often appears alongside that of H.H. Birley on committees including the Provisional Committee of the Liverpool & Manchester Railway.

Henry Garnett began his career by working for his father's and uncle's firm but later changed to trading in iron, a line of business that might have led to commercial dealings with the Bridgewater Foundry. More certain is that his father, Robert Garnett, who held a number of important railway directorships, made efforts to assist the business of Nasmyths Gaskell & Co. It may have been due to his influence as director and principal investor that the London & Birmingham Railway decided to order four locomotives from Patricroft in 1845. Any positive contributions made by Henry Garnett to the affairs of the Bridgewater Foundry beyond that of investor are undocumented. Nasmyth referred to Garnett as his 'excellent friend' in his *Autobiography* and claimed that 'the most perfect harmony always existed between us'. In a letter to Nasmyth dated 1877 Henry Garnett stated, 'I shall always to my dying day feel proud that I have ever been connected with such a man as yourself for whom I shall ever entertain the warmest feelings of regards'.[15]

By 1838, the year in which Nasmyths Gaskell & Co. began locomotive manufacture, the firm was perfectly geared to meet the demands of this new line of business. The financial control of the concern was in safe hands, there was an abundance of investment capital which had been deployed to excellent effect in the construction of a custom-designed factory, and the Nasmyth brothers, especially James, were bursting with new engineering ideas. It is hard to imagine how any new industrial venture could have been more favourably situated – the foundations of the firm were secure and well established.

Holbrook Gaskell with his wife Frances Ann Bellhouse. (SLHL)

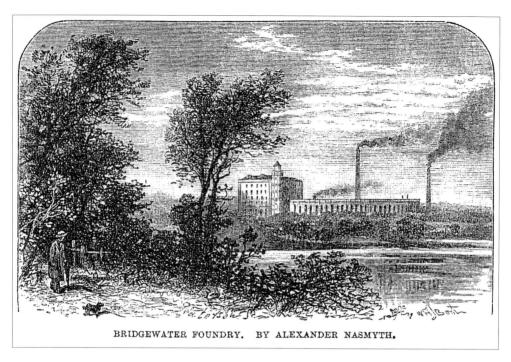

BRIDGEWATER FOUNDRY.   BY ALEXANDER NASMYTH.

Alexander Nasmyth's sketch of the eastern side of the Bridgewater Foundry, c. 1838. (Smiles, 1883)

The Garnett family, 1874. Henry Garnett is seated on the back row in the centre. Stewart Garnett is seated on the steps directly below his father. (Ann Garnett)

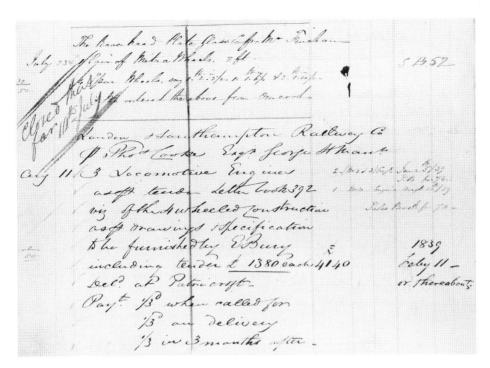

The first Order Book entry for a locomotive contract dated 11 August 1838. (SLHL)

The first surviving locomotive drawing in the Nasmyth archive, c.1838. (Institution of Mechanical Engineers)

three
The Bridgewater Foundry

There were three main phases in the construction and development of the Bridgewater Foundry: the initial building of 1836 and 1837, the extensions of the mid-to-late 1860s and the major expansion programme of the early twentieth century. Until the turn of the century the factory was based on the six-acre site on the western side of Green Lane with the land on the eastern side being used for workers' dwellings. But with the general urbanization and industrialisation of the area west of Manchester and the accompanying growth in working class housing, the factory-owned terraces were demolished to make way for new locomotive-building plant and facilities. For the last quarter century of its existence the Bridgewater Foundry remained substantially the same.

Once the lease for the six-acre site had been signed with Thomas Joseph Trafford in December 1835, work could begin on the new works. The land was 'as flat and neat as a bowling-green' with a 'fine bed of brick-clay' resting upon a solid foundation of sandstone rock. To begin with the business operated from a 'temporary timber workshop' constructed from 'logs of New Brunswick pine'. The machinery from the Dale Street factory flat was transported to Patricroft and Nasmyth claimed that by August 1836 'the Bridgewater Foundry was in complete and efficient action'. As the work increased the workshops were enlarged and wood gave way to brick. This smooth transition from Manchester workshop to Patricroft factory described in the *Autobiography*[1] skates over some of the problems encountered. In one of James Nasmyth's early letters to Holbrook Gaskell, dated 11 July 1836, he deplored the slow progress of Bellhouse, the building contractor, claiming that he had 'behaved very badly'. However, the building was so nearly finished 'as regards the brick work' that it was not feasible to dispense with his services. Despite these teething problems, Nasmyth predicted that 'it will be a noble shop when done' and stated his intention to 'put up another 100ft *all in line* with the present building and employ it as a foundry'.[2]

That the completed Bridgewater Foundry was indeed 'a noble shop' is amply confirmed by two sketches that appeared in the *Autobiography*. These views, together with a contemporary account of the works[3] and the 1848 Ordnance Survey,[4] reveal an overall picture of what amounted to an integrated engineering factory with a comprehensive range of production facilities. At the southern end of the site and overlooking the Liverpool & Manchester Railway, the factory was dominated by the five-storey building already mentioned, which was over 70ft high and measured 100ft long by 60ft wide. The ground floor, with a height of over 20ft, was used as a fitting-up shop. Moving northwards, there was then a line of ground-floor buildings with a total length of 400ft and a uniform width and height of 70 and 21ft respectively. They comprised the planing and heavy turning shops and the main foundry which had a length of 130ft. Behind this were the grinding room, the engine and boiler house, the brass foundry and the ball furnace. Adjacent to these last-named constructions was the smithy. Other buildings existing during the early years were a stable and coach-house, a harness-room and a counting-house on one side of the gateway. The entire complex was designed to facilitate the movement of heavy machinery from one department to another. In order to achieve this the Nasmyths

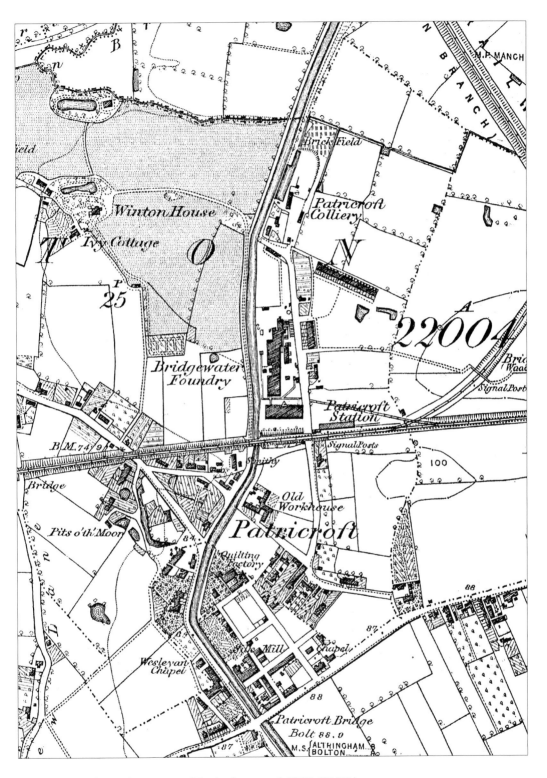

1848 Ordnance Survey map of Patricroft, surveyed 1845. (SLHL)

23

adopted 'the straight line system'. This involved rationalizing the layout of the factory such that work could pass smoothly from one end of the foundry to the other receiving each operation in sequence so minimizing the amount of carrying backwards and forwards or lifting up and down. A railroad was laid through as well as around the shops such that 'any casting, however ponderous or massy, may be removed with the greatest care, rapidity, and security'.

All the machinery and equipment in the new factory was self-produced and included 'fifty-six turning lathes, of all sizes', together with machines for planing, drilling, punching and shearing, key-grooving, plate-bending, shaping and nut-cutting. The first sales book records the production of two foundry cranes, a weighing beam and scales, a carriage and railway for the cupola and a wharf crane. By June 1838 the value of this plant was recorded as £8,885 while that of the buildings was £20,404.[5] The combined effect of the buildings and machinery was one of the most extensive, well-equipped and up-to-date engineering works in the country. It was a custom-built, factory showpiece provided with every facility for the large-scale production of machine tools, steam engines and locomotives. Furthermore, the semi-rural location meant that the works were 'surrounded on all sides with green fields' and the westerly winds provided 'a very long lease of pure air'.[6]

The Bridgewater Foundry was conceived as a general engineering factory and the plant was designed according to function rather than product. Hence the manufacture of locomotives took place alongside the production of steam hammers, stationary steam engines, machine tools and other engineering goods. This made sense since while the demand for engineering products was quite buoyant during the first twenty years or so of the firm's existence, the demand for any particular type of machine was unpredictable. It would have been wasteful building specialist premises for locomotive construction when the latter took place in only thirteen of the first twenty-three years of trading. Specialist locomotive production facilities did begin to appear, however, from the late 1860s, perhaps reflecting a determination amongst the working partners to reap profits from the development of railway networks across the British Empire. Hence an 1867 report on the factory that appeared in a leading technical journal commented that the firm has 'recently recommenced the manufacture of locomotive engines, for which class of work considerable extensions and additions of buildings and plant are now being made'.[7]

These extensions and additions which 'added considerably to the house room and manufacturing facilities of an already first-class concern' comprised a new foundry and turning-shop, a smithy and erecting shop. The foundry was located in a rectangular building 84ft long by 71ft wide with walls 25ft high supporting a wooden roof. A principal feature was a set of four large wrought-iron pillar cranes, each of which was capable of carrying 20 tons and was placed within the building 'in symmetrical position so as to form the four corners of a smaller rectangular figure inscribed within the plan of the building parallel to its outer walls'. The jib of each crane turned in a circle covering the quarter of the foundry in which it was placed and all four jibs could be brought together towards the centre of the foundry. The foundry was served by six cupolas 'some of which are constructed on Mr Ireland's plan' and could melt up to 7 tons of cast iron per hour.[8] A report dated 1894 stated that the foundry was still equipped with Nasmyth's safety ladle 'nothing better having as yet been designed'.[9] The new foundry was called the 'top foundry' indicating its northerly location and had the capacity to produce a 50-ton casting. Indeed, the 50-ton steam hammer for the Woolwich Arsenal was cast here. The capacity of the original, smaller foundry was 12-15 tons.[10]

The new turning or machine shop consisted of two spans of 38ft and 48ft with a common length of 102ft.[11] Light was provided by skylights and additional side windows in the case of the smaller shop. The shafting was driven from a pair of vertical engines having a pair of large pulleys fixed to their crank shaft instead of a fly-wheel. The machines were placed in parallel rows

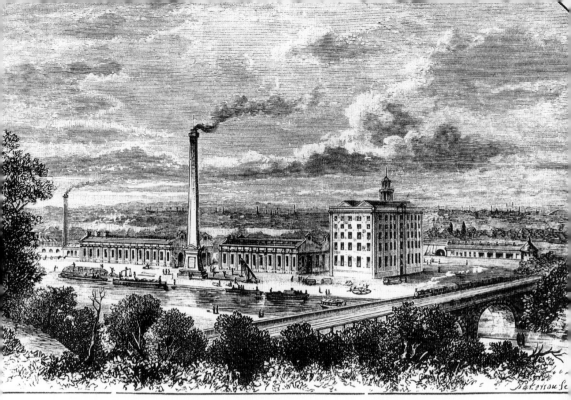

BRIDGEWATER FOUNDRY, PATRICROFT.   FROM A PAINTING BY ALEXANDER NASMYTH.

The Bridgewater Foundry by Alexander Nasmyth, c.1838. (Smiles,1883)

The five-storey building and the Queen's Arms from Patricroft Station, c.1960.
(Frank Mullineux Collection)

lengthways at both sides of the buildings so as to provide a wide space throughout the length of the shop for the movement of work in progress. The smaller lathes were placed back-to-back in double rows such that the workmen could stand face-to-face having the machines between them. Each span was traversed by a travelling crane capable of reaching every tool in the shop. The cranes were worked by hand from below by means of endless cords passing round grooved pulleys attached to the gearing. The crane rails were supported on horizontal cast-iron brackets secured to the side columns with their free ends suspended from the cross beams of the roof. This arrangement, which avoided the use of vertical columns for supporting the longitudinal timbers which carried the crane rails, facilitated the movement of heavy masses within the shop. At time of completion all the tools were made on the premises and particular attention was paid to the accuracy and construction of the teeth for the gearing so promoting steadiness and freedom from vibration particularly in the working of large machines. These new machine shops supplemented the existing heavy machine shop which was heated by steam passing through cast-iron pipes coiled around the structural columns, an idea introduced by Nasmyth.[12]

The new erecting shop measured 120ft by 70ft and was equipped with two travelling cranes supported on hollow rectangular columns. It was located adjacent to the 'mill building'. The smith's shop had the capacity for about fifty fires. Unfortunately there are no detailed contemporary descriptions of these workshops though an account of the factory dated 1887 refers to the smithy, which at that date was divided into two parts, the top and the bottom shop.[13] The latter contained sixteen fires and several steam hammers some of which could deliver 280 blows per minute. The top smithy, for the heavier class of work, contained three steam hammers and fifteen fires. This account also notes that part of the ground floor of the 'mill building' was used for locomotive frame-work and forcing locomotive wheels upon their axles by hydraulic power. Connection with the new erecting shops was through a 'small place' known as the 'Saloon', where there were several large and heavy tools of the kind required for locomotive building.

Between the new buildings described in the technical journals for 1867 and the major expansion programme of the early twentieth century came the construction of a boiler shop at the northern end of the works. This is shown clearly on the Ordnance Survey of 1888 and briefly described in the 1887 account. It comprised a building in two bays each fitted with an overhead crane. The department was capable of accommodating boilers 30ft long and 7ft in diameter and the tools included a range of drilling machines – drilling holes in boiler plates was becoming more common than punching – together with 'exceptionally powerful shears' and MacColl's patent hydraulic riveters. Power was provided by a horizontal condensing engine made by the firm and fitted with Robert Wilson's patent cut-off gear. The completion of the boiler shop necessitated an extension of the railroad which, by 1888, ran all around the works and connected with the London & North Western Railway. At the northern end of the works a travelling crane spanned the canal, while at the opposite end another crane could travel the length of the yard between the machine shops and the 'mill building' ready to lift heavy weights that could not travel by rail onto the canal barges. Virtually every inch of available space had now been developed on the site bounded by the railway, the canal and the road. Further expansion could now take place only by looking to the land to the east of Green Lane where many of the company's employees were housed in five blocks of terraced dwellings.

The Bridgewater Foundry was originally built as a general engineering concern and many of the early locomotive manufacturers – Sharp Roberts, Fairbairns, Hick & Rothwell, etc. – were also general engineers. Specialist locomotive manufacturing firms came into being from the mid-nineteenth century – Beyer Peacock (1855), Manning Wardle (1859), Hudswell & Clarke (1861), Dubs (1865), etc. – with plant and premises designed for a specific purpose. By the 1880s locomotive building was becoming the most important element of Nasmyth Wilson's business and in order to keep abreast of the competition the company authorised a major rebuilding and expansion programme during the first decade of the new century. The first building to be completed was a three-storey, red brick office block facing Green Lane from the east and directly opposite the old machine shops.[14] The ground floor covering an area of 155ft by 43ft provided general office space[15] while the first floor was used as a drawing office with the top floor providing facilities for printing and storage.[16]

The most impressive new buildings on the eastern side of Green Lane were the erecting shop and machine building, a new boiler shop and a painting and packing shop. A correspondent of *The Railway Gazette* found the erecting shop and machine bay as 'probably the most extensively equipped for its purpose that the writer has visited'. The building consisted of a main bay

The Bridgewater Foundry, 1957. (SLHL)

The 1860s new machine shop, 1901. (SLHL)

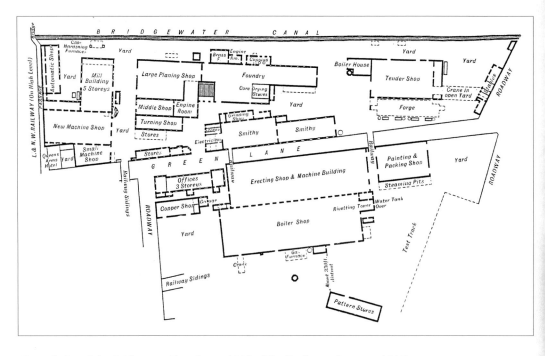

*General plan of the Bridgewater Foundry, c. 1913. (*The Railway Gazette, *1913)*

*The three-storey office block. (*The Railway Gazette, *1913)*

*The foundry. (*The Railway Gazette*, 1913)*

measuring 60ft by 280ft with a height of 50ft with cranes on two levels. The lower level, 24ft above the floor, carried two 5-ton cranes, and the upper level, 32ft above the floor, two 40-ton cranes capable of lifting a complete locomotive. The centre of the bay provided space for a wheel pit and a weighing pit. The side bay measured 32ft by 282ft with a height of 40ft and was fitted with two 5-ton cranes. The building was equipped with drills, grinders, a plate slotting machine and a polishing plant. The adjoining boiler shop had two bays with a common height and length of 50ft and 284ft respectively and widths of 50ft and 36ft. Crane gantries were provided 24ft from the floor level with a 5-ton electric crane in the small bay and two 15-ton electric cranes in the large bay. The boiler shop was also serviced by a riveting tower, a Siemens gas furnace, an accumulator and pumps for working the flanging press, a staving press and other machinery. The high-speed drills, shears and punches, rolls, saws and edge planers together with the portable riveters, pneumatic plant and compressed air service for hammers and caulkers, amounted to equipment 'of the most complete character that it is possible to imagine'.

The painting and packing shop consisted of two bays each 35ft by 105ft with a height of 40ft. Both bays were equipped with electric cranes 'to enable stripping to be carried out'. Other facilities included a modern heating and drying plant, weighbridges and two steaming

*The forge. (*The Railway Gazette, *1913)*

Automatic machine shop.
(The Railway Gazette, 1913)

Heavy motion machine shop.
(The Railway Gazette, 1913)

Machine bay of boiler shop.
(The Railway Gazette, *1913)*

*Boiler shop looking towards riveting tower. (*The Railway
Gazette, *1913)*

Boilers awaiting dispatch. (SLHL)

pits with adjustable rollers for all gauges located outside the shop on the eastern side. The pits were protected by an overhanging roof and ventilated by telescopic chimneys. Apart from a pattern store the other new building on the eastern site was the copper shop, located behind the offices and provided with tools and ventilating apparatus. All the new buildings described were electrically illuminated by arc lamps together with independent lights for each vice and tool.

While most of the new building took place on the seven-acre site on the eastern side of Green Lane, there were also conversions, reorganisations and rebuilding on the original western site which was connected to the new premises at three points by three lines of railway which had right of way across the road. The main foundry, smithy, machine shops and 'mill building' remained in place, but the original boiler shop was rebuilt or converted into a tender shop. The forge and engine room were reconstructed and, at the southern end of the site, a new machine shop and small machine shop were created from the space released from the original locomotive erecting shed. An automatic shop was also added. The tender shop measured 137ft by 74ft with a height of 25ft and the tools included side planer, shears, punches, drills, rolls and a steam hammer. The forge, 140ft by 27ft with a height of 30ft, housed four regenerative furnaces for producing steam for the three steam hammers. Heavy forgings were moved by jib cranes and the forge worked continuously to meet the regular demand for engine cranks. The engine room, reconstructed in 1911, housed a superheated steam, cross-compound, horizontal, semi-slow speed engine built by Musgraves & Sons of Bolton with a motor-driven surface condenser.

Coppersmith's shop. (The Railway Gazette, *1913)*

A Dick Kerr generator was mounted directly onto the engine shaft to supply the electric current for providing the power throughout the factory.

The new machine shop immediately adjoining the mill building had two bays each 35ft by 140ft with a height of 23ft and each equipped with a 5-ton electric crane. On one side of this building was a small machine shop, 70ft by 38ft with a height of 15ft and an auxiliary gas engine drive to enable this part of the works to remain operative during holiday periods and breakdowns. The automatic machine shop in the south western corner of the site, measuring 102ft by 31ft 6in with a height of 25ft, contained a variety of automatic tools including screwing machines, turret lathes and nut-making machinery. It also provided space for a testing department. Materials entering or leaving the works were scrutinized by a 50-ton hydraulic testing machine manufactured by Joshua Buckton & Co.

When the Bridgewater Foundry was first built all the tools and equipment were made on the premises and a considerable trade was conducted in the sale of machine tools and forge and foundry apparatus. Even at the time of the 1867 extensions it was noted that all the tools in

Erecting shop showing 2-8-0 locomotives for India under construction. (The Railway Gazette, 1913)

Erecting shop showing 2-8-0 locomotives for India under construction. (The Railway Gazette, 1913)

This page and opposite:*The erecting shop during the interwar period. (SLHL)*

the machine shop were 'made by the firm for their own use'.[17] By 1894 the old Nasmyth tools – such as the wheel-cutting machine, slot drill and shaper – were working alongside copper stay and stud machines by Kendall & Gent and tools designed by Muir, Whitworth and others.[18] By 1913 the displacement of in-house tools and equipment was almost complete. The electric cranes were built by specialist suppliers – Craven Brothers, Higginbottom & Mannock, Vaughan & Sons, J. Berry and J. Spencer & Co. Similarly, the machine tools were provided, in the main, by the leading British manufacturers of the period such as John Holroyd & Co. (axle lathes), Armstrong, Whitworth & Co. (slotting machines and a 24in centre lathe), Clifton & Waddell (sawing machines), Smith & Coventry (slot drilling machines), Alfred Herbert (pin drill and boiler stay automatic machine) and Brown & Sharpe (milling machine). Nasmyth Wilson could no longer be considered amongst their number. The only home-produced tool worthy of mention, apart from the steam hammers, was a patent copper stay riveter invented by the works manager, James Bolas.[19] This was in use in the riveting tower and impressed with the speed of its action and the quality of work performed. Leakage from stays riveted with this tool was 'practically unknown'. Otherwise the firm was dependent upon outside suppliers, even for such products as the foundry-blowing engine which was constructed by Tannett & Walker.

Armed with the best designed equipment and tools and the more spacious and well appointed shops, Nasmyth Wilson could reasonably claim to have one of the most advantageously planned locomotive factories in the country. *The Railway Gazette* of 1913 confidently claimed that the works 'as at presently constituted, rank among the most important and best equipped of any engaged in the production of locomotives' and that the remodelled works were quite capable of 'producing locomotives on a large scale and of all sizes and types'. It is ironic that within two years of the composition of these words the outbreak of war would help to destroy the world markets which provided the basis of the prosperity of the firm. With the steady fall in custom during the inter-war period there was no need for further development of the factory premises and the 1938 Ordnance Survey of the works shows a layout virtually identical to the plan published in 1913. The demise of Nasmyth Wilson had little to do with inadequate production facilities. The Bridgewater Foundry was always in the vanguard of factory design and equipment.

*The engine room. (*The Railway Gazette, *1913)*

*Motor-driven hydraulic wheel press. (*The Railway Gazette, *1913)*

Opposite: *The erecting shop during the interwar period. (SLHL)*

four
Workforce

The displacement of traditional skills by machine tools meant that there were major changes in the composition of the workforce at the Bridgewater Foundry between 1838 and 1938. Semi and unskilled labourers largely replaced skilled craftsmen. This was not a gradual change but came in fits and starts. The major innovatory periods, relating to the introduction of labour saving devices, were between the establishment of the firm and 1845 and during the late 1880s and early 1890s. Both these periods, which reflected developments across the engineering industry, were followed by major national strikes, in 1852 and 1897/98.

By 1838 most of the basic types of machine tool – the lathe, planing machine, drill and slotter – had reached a stage that was to remain substantially the same for the next forty years. Nasmyth improved many of the existing designs and added a number of specialist tools for executing detailed work such as the shaper and nut-miller. Most of these tools performed work previously undertaken by hand such that those versed in the arts of the chisel, hammer and file were no longer needed in such numbers. The machine tool technology obviously posed a threat to craft workers who wished to preserve their privileged status and superior rates of pay. This process formed the backcloth for a number of bitter contests between Nasmyth and sections of his workforce. By contrast, the Wilson years, 1857 to 1882, were relatively calm as there were no major technological challenges to the balance between capital and labour. The 1890s, however, saw the introduction of a new generation of machine tools such as turret lathes, milling machines and precision grinding machines which served to speed-up production processes and gave added prominence to semi-skilled machine minders in place of the fitters and turners. Piece-work began to replace time rates as the firm sought to maximize the productivity of the new machinery. Industrial relations were less harmonious at the Bridgewater Foundry during the new century until the threat of closure and unemployment undermined the bargaining power of engineering workers.

There are numerous references to the size of the workforce at the Bridgewater Foundry. By 1839 employees numbered around 300 and by 1842 this figure had grown to 500. Nasmyth claimed that the highest number of workmen he employed was 1,500.[1] Robert Wilson is described in the 1861 census as the employer of 176 men and 50 boys and, ten years later, of 203 men and 30 boys. For 22 years between 1883 and 1911 the records of the Locomotive Manufacturers Association include reported workforce numbers. These show that Nasmyth Wilson employed between 300 and 706 persons at the beginning and end of the period respectively with an average of 450. By contrast numbers at Beyer Peacock varied between 1,196 (1895) and 2,789 (1908) while those for North British varied between 6,216 (1910) and 7,999 (1907).[2] A brief description of the Patricroft works, dated June 1929, stated that about 700 workmen were normally employed at Nasmyth's.[3] The 1930s depression must have brought about major lay-offs though there are no records of the size of the workforce during the worst affected years. At all times the workforce would have continually expanded and contracted according to the level of orders and only the most highly skilled, responsible and valued workers would have had any kind of security of employment.

Foundry workers with James Bolas, works manager, c.1900. (SLHL)

Forge workers with James Bolas, works manager, c.1900. (SLHL)

BRIDGEWATER FOUNDRY.

Dining Room Regulations.

The Directors of Messrs. Nasmyth, Wilson & Co., Ltd., have recently re-fitted, enlarged, and considerably improved the Dining Room in connection with these works, and provision has been made for accommodating rather over 160 workmen for either breakfast or dinner.

It has been the practice of the firm in the past to make a small charge of 2d. a week towards the expenses of this Dining Room, but it has been decided for the future to make no charge for the use of the Room. As, however, it has been modernized and re-fitted at considerable cost, it is specially requested that all using it will observe certain necessary regulations, having for their object the maintenance of cleanliness and order.

The services of Female Attendants will be provided by the firm for brewing tea, coffee, or cocoa, boiling eggs, and for warming up food already cooked, but beyond this no other cooking will be undertaken.

It is the opinion of the Directors that it will be best for the Dining Room to be under the control of a Chairman or President and Committee elected by the workmen from among themselves, and further, that only adult workmen and not apprentices should be eligible to vote for the election of this Committee.

In each of the time offices a rack will be provided in which suitable cans will be placed, numbered consecutively. These cans are the property of the firm and must on no account be removed from the premises.

Dining room regulations, 1914. (SLHL)

It appears that there was little problem in assembling the original workforce and Nasmyth recalls in his *Autobiography* how Worsley village, the headquarters of the Bridgewater Canal, supplied him with a valuable number of workmen 'accustomed to the heaviest class of work' in connection with the on and off-loading of goods. There was an abundance of skilled labour to be found in south Lancashire and Cheshire and Nasmyth claimed that their mechanical instincts had been acquired through the generations from the Norman smiths and armourers introduced into the locality by Hugo de Lupus, chief armourer to William the Conqueror.[4] This native workforce was soon to be diluted, however, by the arrival of 'sixty-four first-rate men' from Scotland imported by Nasmyth to resolve his first experience of strike action at the Bridgewater Foundry which occurred in November 1836. These men were later followed by their brothers, nephews and cousins such that Scotsmen made up a major portion of the new work force. A number of the early works managers and foremen also had Scottish connections including Archie Torry, Robert Wilson, Robert Willis and James Hutton.

Working conditions in any nineteenth century engineering factory were dangerous. There was a constant risk of injury from the molten iron in the foundry, metal fragments in the machine shops and heavy articles transported by cranes across the erecting sheds. It was in response to the first of these dangers that Nasmyth devised his safety foundry ladle which minimized the risk of 'frightful scalds and burns'. Even senior members of the firm were not immune and Holbrook Gaskell took early retirement following an accident when he was struck on the head by a falling beam in the foundry.[5] A cursory insight into some of the minor injuries sustained during the

Female employees during the First World War (Minnie Roberts on left). (SLHL)

Employees in erecting and boiler shops. (SLHL)

1840s and 1850s is provided by the firm's day book which recorded petty cash expenditure. Here are found entries for the purchase of brandy 'from Thorndykes for Labrs Leg broken in Foundry' and 'Leeches for Pollit who was hurt by the falling of the remainder of the old Boiler Shed Roof'. In April 1851, a moulder named John Atherton 'who burnt his foot in the Foundry last July – unable to work since – now going to Southport', was given a gift of five shillings.[6]

The most serious incident that took place at the Bridgewater Foundry was a boiler explosion which occurred in 1845. This calamitous event which resulted from 'an over-pressure of steam, produced by the water having been allowed to get too low in the boiler' resulted in the deaths of an engineman and fitter, serious burns to a hammer operator and minor cuts, scalds and burns to many other workmen. A five-year-old child, the son of John Hepworth, foreman of the boiler makers, had his skull fractured by a falling slate while playing in the garden. The casualty list would have been much longer but for the fact that the incident occurred during the dinner hour which removed about forty men from the range of the explosion. In the absence of health and safety legislation the victims of such tragedies were eligible for little more than charitable gestures. Hence the widow of Henry Davies, the fitter who had received fatal injuries to his thigh from part of an uprooted 3-ton steam hammer, received a donation from the firm of 5s 3½d so making her deceased husband's wages up to a round pound.[7]

At the time of the boiler explosion the firm summoned medical assistance from physicians and surgeons in Croft Bank and Eccles but the nearest hospital to the factory was the Manchester Royal Infirmary. The seriously wounded were transported there by coaches and an omnibus. In subsequent years, access to medical treatment substantially improved with the opening of the Eccles and Patricroft Hospital in the late 1890s. In September 1898 the local newspaper records the admission of a young machine minder, Herbert Pendlebury, with a badly crushed wrist while in September 1907 William Wood was treated for a crushed foot having been conveyed by the borough horse ambulance.[8] More immediate attention was provided by a local doctor, who treated James Derbyshire when he lost two fingers on a slotting machine in 1884,[9] and one of the foremen with first aid expertise. The latter, T.E. Pinches, had treated 400 cases by the end of 1902 'many of a serious nature'.[10]

The living environment around the Bridgewater Foundry was originally semi-rural and Nasmyth wrote of the 'many picturesque old farmhouses and cottages' embraced by 'pure air' and set in the 'fresh, free, open country' which promoted the good health of his workforce and their families.[11] But as the area became increasingly industrialised so the problems of pollution, disease and inadequate drainage began to undermine the former advantages of the location. The 1851 Board of Health enquiry into the sanitary state of Barton-upon-Irwell drew attention to the prevalence of cholera, fever, overcrowding, defective water supply, open cesspools, unpaved streets and middens and pigsties in unhealthy proximity to human habitations.[12] Nasmyth's workforce must all have suffered from the lack of adequate amenities which properly required the application of the Public Health Act, an application which, as one of the major ratepayers, Nasmyth vigorously opposed.[13]

The firm did take steps, however, to provide suitable dwellings for at least some of its employees. By 1839 the number of cottages and houses stood at forty-two and this had risen to eighty-nine by 1850. Each dwelling commanded a weekly rent of 3s which was deducted from wages. This residential property was situated on the eastern side of Green Lane and was arranged in four terraces: Foremen's Row, Boiler Makers' Row, Long Row and Railway Terrace. This workers cottage community included a shop and a small library which by 1845 contained some 500 volumes when the firm donated it to the recently established Mechanics Institute at Patricroft.[14] Drinkwater's field at the side of Patricroft Station provided the ground for a cricket club associated with the Bridgewater Foundry during the 1870s.[15] Unfortunately, the factory community had

Unidentified employee on locomotive footplate. (SLHL)

to be broken up during the early 1900s to release land for the construction of extensions to the works. These extensions did provide, however, for a foundry dining room which by 1914 could accommodate 160 workmen and was managed by an elected chairman and committee.

During the 1830s the working day at the Bridgewater Foundry began at 6 a.m. and when orders were pressing might continue until 10 p.m. Albert Platts who joined Nasmyth's in 1906 at the age of thirteen was expected to work a fifty-three hour week. Employees were expected to work six days a week for fifty-two weeks in the year. Wage rates varied considerably according to the capability of the workman. In the 1830s these ranged between 3s a week for 'clever lads' to up to 24s a week for skilled mechanics. Albert Platts was expected to work his first month 'for nothing' and then began on 4s a week. Apprentices in the early twentieth century received a shilling increase on their birthday receiving 14s when they came out of time. Overtime was denied to anyone under the age of eighteen.[16]

The employees were supervised by a hierarchy of foremen, general works manager and working partner or director. The foremen were expected to be 'of active habits & capable of enforcing activity in others'. Nasmyth appreciated their worth and ensured that they had never 'cause to look over the hedge'. It was the task of the general works manager to coordinate the work of the different departments and ensure that no one doubted his managerial competence. Nasmyth wrote to Robert Wilson in 1856:

Stir up every department by your presence and by oversight into every hole and corner, let your eye be felt as well as seen by every man and boy in the place there's nothing like it to keep them all up to the mark.[17]

At no time were the attitudes and labour policies adopted by the Bridgewater Foundry proprietors as uncompromising as they were during the early years. Nasmyth was determined to remain the unquestioned master in his own works and this involved an almost total disregard of the various union restrictions on the training, promotion and wage bargaining of engineering workers. His attitude towards union-organised labour was one of non-recognition, arguing that there was a separate contract of employment between him and every individual employee and that the relations between employer and employed should be based on the principles of free trade without the intervention of third parties. He generally refused to receive deputations representing the workmen's common interests, arguing that if an employee was dissatisfied with his lot he was free to remove his labour elsewhere. Writing shortly after the strike of 1852, Nasmyth referred to the Amalgamated Society of Engineers as 'the amalgamated scoundrills' who were involved in a 'monster conspiracy' against the 'natural rights of Employment & Labour'. He claimed that the proof that engineering workers were quite adequately paid could be seen in 'the loads of food they gorge themselves with' and that complaints of 'excessive labour' which denied the men time to 'cultivate their minds' were, in reality, demands for more time in which to consume 'ale & tobacco'.[18] Nasmyth took particular exception to the apprenticeship system which he condemned as 'the fag end of the feudal system' and advocated its abolition 'in every branch of business'. Instead he adopted a policy of employing 'intelligent well-conducted young lads' who were then advanced according to their merits.[19] This preference was made possible by the increased deployment of self-acting tools which required superintendence rather than labouring.

Given the technological context and Nasmyth's own approach to labour relations it is hardly surprising that there were a number of strikes at the Bridgewater Foundry during the first twenty years of its existence. The first occurred before locomotive manufacture began in 1836 and concerned the partners' readiness to give employment to a former strike breaker and two men who had not served a formal apprenticeship. Reference has already been made to how Nasmyth 'Scotched' this strike by importing replacement labour from Glasgow, Aberdeen and Dundee. But news of Nasmyth's tactics soon spread throughout the engineering workshops of Britain such that the new recruits were confined to working at Patricroft for the rest of their working lives. Hence Nasmyth was only able to preserve his right to employ the working men of his choice by restricting the employment prospects of those very same workmen outside of his own factory. The second strike occurred in August 1842 and formed part of the alleged 'General Strike' of that year, more commonly known as 'The Great Plug Plot Riots'. Little is known relating to the involvement of Nasmyth's workers in this event beyond the fact that David Morrison was a leading activist in the troubles, being one of the delegates to the 'Great Delegate Trades Conference' held on 15 and 16 August 1842, as well as a defendant in the trial of Feargus O'Connor and fifty-eight others. Given the poor trading prospects of 1842 the firm would almost certainly have been compelled to reduce wages. Nasmyth's final contest with the union-organised sections of his workforce came with the 1852 Lock Out. Hibbert & Platt of Oldham, faced with union opposition to their practices of overtime working, piece-work and the employment of 'illegal' men, made common cause with other engineering firms in both Lancashire and London. Since Nasmyth was already violating a number of union restrictions he became a willing member of this alliance. Some 300 men were refused entry to the factory between January and March though non-union men were kept in full employment. Nasmyth used the opportunity to increase his quota of 'unbound apprentices' and the deployment of self-acting machines.[20]

The 'Wilson years' were a time of relative calm in the relations between employers and workmen and at the Bridgewater Foundry this was helped by Wilson's own more conciliatory

Employees with thirty years or more service, 1944. (SLHL)

approach to employment issues. He reintroduced a form of apprenticeship and on at least one occasion provided a high tea for his workforce during which he made a speech emphasizing the benefits of self-education above the temptations provided by the public house. The local newspaper judged that such occasions were beneficial for 'diminishing the distance... between employer and employed'.[21] Whereas Nasmyth had spent his recreational hours engaged in astronomy or painting, Wilson played an active community role assuming the chair of the Patricroft Mechanics Institute and involving himself in the local churches and the Eccles Freemasons Lodge.[22]

The period between the late 1890s and the mid-1920s saw renewed industrial conflict at Patricroft. The national 1897-1898 lock-out was essentially a re-run of the points at issue in 1852 – a test case regarding the enforcement of engineering employers' prerogatives with regard to restrictive practices and the control of machinery.[23] The union defeat led to more than a decade of relative peace. Then in January 1912 Bridgewater Foundry apprentices joined 5,000 others in the Manchester area in an unsuccessful strike for a pay rise.[24] During the First World War there were minor disagreements over the 'dilution' of the skilled workforce[25] and the introduction of female labour but there was no further strike action until the national disputes of 1921 and 1926. The union failure in both campaigns had a sobering effect on the Nasmyth workforce and there was reluctance to become involved with the 1930 strike in pursuit of an 8s a week pay rise.[26] The depressed trade of the 1930s meant that fear of unemployment became the dominant economic issue and the final years of trading at the Bridgewater Foundry witnessed no further contests between employers and workmen.

five

The Nasmyth Locomotive Contracts
1838-1853

James Nasmyth was the managing partner at the Bridgewater Foundry for twenty-one years, from 1836 to 1856. During this time 109 steam locomotives were built at the factory. Four engines were sent abroad. Sales records are complete from 1837 until Nasmyth's retirement and these show that total locomotive and tender revenues amounted to approximately £231,000. This figure represents over a quarter of the aggregate sales for the period 1837 to 1856. The other components of revenue were steam hammers, thirty-two per cent, and stationary steam engines, machine tools and miscellaneous engineering equipment, forty-three per cent. The Bridgewater Foundry benefited from the railway industry in other ways during this period for many of the newly established railway company workshops notably Swindon, Wolverton, Crewe and Nine Elms, placed orders for machinery and equipment as did some of the private locomotive manufacturers such as Beyer Peacock and The Vulcan Foundry. The London & North Western Railway received fourteen Nasmyth steam hammers before the end of 1856 and Sharp Stewart received nine. The benefit from the railway workshops was two-edged, however, and Nasmyth claimed that their establishment and the consequent demand for new labour drove up wage rates significantly.[1]

Locomotive manufacture at the Bridgewater Foundry under Nasmyth can be divided into two phases – the opening phase of 1838 to 1842 and the second phase of 1845 to 1853. The years when no locomotive building took place do not necessarily imply any shortcomings on the part of the firm. The formation of railway companies that followed the success of the Liverpool & Manchester Railway soon led to a rapid increase in demand for locomotives which peaked in 1840 when an estimated 279 engines were built.[2] There was then a temporary but sharp fall in investment with the numbers of locomotives ordered falling by more than half by 1843. By the latter date the first of the railway company workshops were building locomotives and the Bridgewater Foundry was also having to compete with more than a dozen leading manufacturers. Profit margins would have been slim and even the prospect of foreign contracts had to be handled with circumspection. Nasmyth records how in 1842 he visited Nuremberg with Holbrook Gaskell in order to tender for locomotives for the Nuremberg-Munich Railway. Despite 'tempting commercial blandishments' the two partners found it 'imprudent' to agree to the terms of the contract on account of 'riskful conditions' and returned home empty handed.[3] During the final three years of Nasmyth's involvement with the firm the absence of locomotive business may have had something to do with the buoyant state of steam hammer production. Nasmyth was understandably keen to maximize the profits of the firm in the immediate run-up to his early retirement and profit margins on steam hammers would have been substantially above those available from locomotive contracts since the steam hammer was protected by patent until the end of 1856.[4] It is possible, therefore, that Nasmyth declined to accept locomotive orders.

During the first phase of locomotive building at the Bridgewater Foundry, 1838 to 1842, orders were received for forty-six engines. All but four were from the mainline domestic railway companies – London & Southampton, Manchester & Leeds, Midland Counties, Birmingham

47

Engineering products manufactured at the Bridgewater Foundry invented or improved by James Nasmyth;
Above left: *Model of steam hammer engine. (SLHL)*
Above right: *Slotting machine. (SLHL)*
Below left: *Shaping machine. (SLHL)*
Below right: *Ambidexter lathe. (SLHL)*

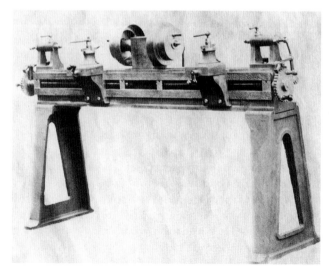

& Gloucester and the Great Western. Two locomotives were exported to Austria and another two, named *Nasmyth* and *Patricroft*, were sold for industrial use at Darwen Mills, Blackburn.[5] The dealings between Nasmyths Gaskell and their early locomotive customers are the best documented in the history of the firm since the business letter books are complete for the period 1838-1840. These books provide an interesting insight into the often problematic relationship between private builder and railway company, especially with regard to financial and technical arrangements and the surprisingly ill-defined nature of the original contracts which inevitably gave rise to misunderstandings. They also lend weight to the arguments in favour of the major companies deciding to construct their own rolling stock. The detail with which the earliest contracts can be considered cannot be repeated for the later contracts on account of the destruction of much of the source material.[6]

The first steam locomotive manufactured by Nasmyth's was an experimental engine, a 2-2-2 on Stephenson's principle, appropriately named *Bridgewater*. This was 'similar to some of the Best Engines on the Li'pool & Mancr Railway' and was offered to a number of prospective purchasers for £1,450.[7] It obviously made sense to obtain some experience of locomotive building before accepting orders from the railway companies. But *Bridgewater* was more than a prototype. It represented an attempt by Nasmyth to take the lead in locomotive manufacture by offering stock items for sale. In 1836 he had written to Gaskell about his ideas for achieving a 'ready-made concern'[8] and had soon been able to offer a number of the smaller machine tools – nut cutting machines, wall drilling machines, for example – from stock. Locomotives were an entirely different matter, however, both on account of their capital value and the fact that railway companies usually had very particular ideas concerning the specifications of their rolling stock. In total, Nasmyths Gaskell & Co. manufactured four locomotives without first obtaining orders.[9] Reference is made to them in a number of letters including one to Henry Garnett's father:

We have three very perfect engines making in stock. *They are 14in cylinders and embody every improvement which we have made and which has resulted from our former experience. Should you hear of any company who would be likely to require such we should esteem it as an especial favour you mentioning them as they can be had on such short notice, it might serve both us and them.*[10]

Judging from the low prices obtained for the stock engines[11] the policy of locomotive stock selling proved a failure and after November 1841 all locomotives produced at the Bridgewater Foundry were made to order.

The first order for locomotive steam engines was received from the London & Southampton Railway in August 1838. This seventy-seven-mile enterprise had been authorized in 1834 and the line opened between 1838 and 1840. It was renamed the London & South Western Railway in 1839, a name it was to retain until the amalgamations of 1923. The coaching interest detractors of the line, which passed through the cathedral city of Winchester, claimed that it had been built for the 'conveyance of parsons and prawns'. It was one of three railway trunk routes out of London at this time, the other two being the projected lines to Birmingham and Bristol. The locomotives were to be built to the designs provided by Edward Bury (1794-1858) of the Clarence Foundry, Liverpool, who was also locomotive superintendent of the London & Birmingham Railway.[12] James Nasmyth had been introduced to Bury in 1834 while trying to decide whether Liverpool or Manchester was to be the location for his business activities[13] and, prior to receiving the locomotive order, had supplied him with a nut-cutting machine.

Detailed negotiations had been taking place between Bury and Henry Garnett during July 1838. It appears that a price higher than the finally agreed £1,380, inclusive of tenders, had been named by the firm and when this was turned down by the Liverpool engineer, Gaskell

A Norris locomotive similar to the six built for Birmingham & Gloucester Railway, NW17 to 19 and 22 to 24, 1840-1. (SLHL)

agreed 'to undertake the Engines at the same prices you are now giving other respectable houses for similar engines'.[14] During a meeting with George Nasmyth, Thomas Cooke, a Manchester director of the railway company, made the decision to order three locomotives from Nasmyths Gaskell & Co. and this led to the firm's formal tender and subsequent acceptance of the contract on 11 August 1838. The engines were to be 'delivered at our works in six months from the confirmation of the order or as near thereto as possible'.[15] In fact, it was over a year before the order was completed. Two engines, the *Hawk* and the *Falcon*, were delivered on 6 July 1839 and the third, *Raven*, was delivered on 20 August 1839.

At least part of the blame for this delay can be attributed to Bury who, in addition to supplying 'the specification and detailed drawings,' was to supply a number of castings and finished parts. It is clear that his late delivery of these items held up the engine production. By the end of October 1838 the firm had already made three requests for some iron and brass castings arguing that it 'is quite impossible that we can keep time when we are so much retarded. Our men are actually at a stand for want of them'.[16] Letters with a similar message were written up to April 1839.

Bury's role was not confined to that of designer and supplier of materials for it was also understood that he was to be used in a consultative capacity and the railway company made a charge on each engine in consideration of this facility. The firm claimed that they used this privilege 'as sparingly as possible' and there are two letters only requesting Bury's technical advice. One concerned a proposed modification to the curve of the springs 'to provide for the deflection which will take place when they are weighted', and the other concerned the method by which the locomotive frames were to be connected with the underguards.[17]

The relationship between Bury and Nasmyths Gaskell & Co. was to prove extremely

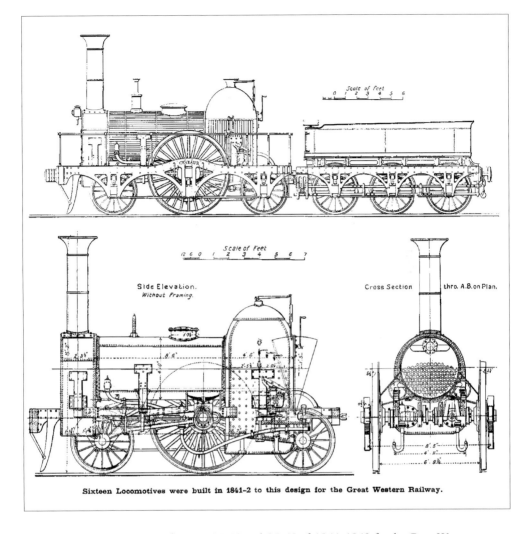

Sixteen Locomotives were built in 1841-2 to this design for the Great Western Railway.

*General arrangement drawings for NW 25-32 and 35-42 of 1841-1842 for the Great Western Railway. (*The Railway Gazette, *1913)*

unsatisfactory to the latter. Not only did Bury disrupt the manufacturing processes by his delays, he also substantially reduced the firm's profits on the contract through his exorbitant charges. When Gaskell received the invoice for the various castings and finished items supplied from Liverpool including glass gauge stands and whistles, he was shocked at the contents:

Iron castings contracted for at 18s 8d per cwt are charged 21s per cwt. But the finished work is overcharged much more seriously. The glass gauge stands for which £5 would be an outside price are charged £10 each. Buffers are charged £10 & we are paying to another party for the very same article £2 5s 0d. There is an item of £3 10s 0d for timber for Bumpers which we cannot in any way account for. Leather Hose pipes £6 12s 0d belong to & came with the Tenders & of course are not chargeable to us. We mention these items only as specimens of the charges but the whole account is overcharged for instance Brass whistles for which we have not been asked more than 21s & can bring lower are charged 40s & Blow off cocks 70s for which we can shew you invoices at 27s[18]

In a later letter Gaskell claimed that Bury's charges were 'so very high' that the firm could not afford to pay them and that if the firm did pay such charges 'we should very soon be ruined'.[19] A revised account was demanded and in the meantime Gaskell ordered a similar set of locomotive mountings from another supplier. When these goods arrived they were not only cheaper than Bury's but superior in quality. Bury remained unimpressed and in an attempt to end the deadlock Gaskell suggested halving the difference or submitting the matter to the arbitration of some mutual friend. When this also failed to appeal to Bury's sense of business propriety, Gaskell reluctantly paid up to avoid the 'trouble & expense of a lawsuit'.[20] The profitability of the contract had also been reduced when Bury requested the tender production to be transferred to his Clarence Foundry for, according to Gaskell, the tenders proved to be the only profitable part of the order.

If the contract with the London & Southampton Railway was less financially remunerative than had been hoped, the dealings with Bury could be put down to experience. What was most important was that the contract should be an engineering success so that the firm could attract further orders. The trial performances of the *Hawk* suggested that this had been achieved, at least in the eyes of the manufacturers:

It ran ... three days on the Lipool & Manchr R'lway – on the first day it merely plied between Chat Moss & Manchester ... on the second day it carried goods from terminus to terminus & made four trips in the course of the day each time carrying heavily laden trains with great expedition – one of these trains consisted of 20 wagons weighing 120 Tons & it took these from L'pool to Manchester in an hour & a quarter including stoppages & on stopping at Parkside on this occasion to take in fuel it was found to have consumed so little of the Coke with which it started from L'pool that there was amply sufficient left to carry the Train to the end of the journey ... On the last day of trial it conveyed four Passenger Trains from one Town to the other & ran with one of them heavily laden ... in 51 minutes and it had been obliged to slacken pace four times in the course of the journey owing to obstructions in the road – it also ascended the Incline with this & the other first class trains which it conveyed – without assistance. On this day it also conveyed a second class train to Manchester in an hour and a quarter having stopped 17 times on the road to take up or deposit Passengers.[21]

Before being sent to the customer via the Grand Junction Railway, the engines were inspected by Bury and Edward Woods of the Liverpool & Manchester Railway. Once delivered to the London & Southampton Railway, the three locomotives initially worked the local train services but were afterwards employed on shunting operations in Nine Elms yard. The *Hawk* and *Falcon* were probably broken up after five or six years as their names were given to two other engines built in 1843. The *Raven* continued marshalling trains for the Richmond line until 1851 when it was withdrawn from traffic and adapted for driving machinery in the shops.[22]

The Midland Counties Railway had purchased one of Nasmyth's stock engines in August 1840. Prior to this in February 1839 the railway company had ordered six passenger locomotives again on Bury's design. Nasmyth's original offer quoted £1,300 per engine but this was subsequently reduced to £1,250 with £180 for the tenders.[23] The directors of the company were obviously quite determined to obtain value for money and it was noted in the order book:

At the option of the Board of Directors the said Engines be liable to rejection or a reduction of £100 in the price of each Engine if not found equal & similar in all respects to the Best Engines made by Mr Bury or Mr Hick for the London & Birmingham Railway.[24]

Other demands were not so reasonable. For example, the company attempted to insert a clause into the contract whereby Nasmyths Gaskell & Co. were not only expected to implement Bury's most recent improvements, such as the welded firebox, but also any technical advances that were 'about to be introduced'. The firm not unnaturally objected to the 'vague & prospective clause' though it agreed to introduce any improvement that did not materially increase the expense of the engines provided adequate notice was granted.[25]

It was most fortunate for the firm that they did not sign the offending clause, for it is clear from a number of letters sent to the railway company that they tried to change the design of the locomotives well after production had begun. In September 1839 the firm expressed regret that the cylinders and pistons had already been bored, turned and finished or they would gladly have made them larger.[26] Again, in January 1840, less than three months before the specified completion date, the railway company was wanting the installed fireboxes to be removed and replaced with copper fireboxes. The firm claimed that such 'a material alteration' would 'almost ruin the Engines'.[27] So far had the railway company's ideas changed on the subject of their rolling stock during the course of 1839 that in November of that year they were prepared to order larger engines from Nasmyths Gaskell & Co. provided the firm could dispose of the locomotives in hand.[28]

Arguments between manufacturer and railway company over the details of engine construction were predictable at a time of prolific technical innovation in the details of locomotive design. The firm was again involved in a series of misunderstandings, this time with the Manchester & Leeds Railway, regarding the type of wheel centres to be fitted on the three locomotives ordered by that company in August 1838. The specifications prepared by George Stephenson were loosely worded and in the absence of any instructions to the contrary, Nasmyth used cast-iron when, in fact, Stephenson wanted wrought-iron instead. Nasmyths Gaskell & Co. made a number of appeals to the company's chief engineer, Thomas Gooch, claiming that they were so convinced of the 'efficiency & safety' of the wheels that they were prepared to 'stake our professional reputation upon their success'.[29] Gooch made a personal inspection of the offending articles and apparently thought well of them but the final decision rested with Stephenson who refused to alter his position. Nasmyths Gaskell & Co. then claimed £100 per engine as compensation for the cost of making the alterations and the company directors eventually agreed to pay half this amount.[30]

The three locomotives, *Rochdale*, *Bradford* and *Hull*, were delivered in July and September 1839. The first two were used for the Rochdale traffic but the fate of the third is lamented in a letter to John Todd, the superintendent of the company's locomotive department. Apparently the *Hull* had been sentenced to the railway's 'back settlements' and was being used for 'ballasting'. The firm appealed for 'a commutation of her sentence' so that she could 'run with her colleagues'.[31] It is unclear whether or not this request was granted but certainly the engines were sufficiently successful to induce the company to place an order for two additional locomotives and in January 1841 the *Derby* and *Sheffield* were delivered to the line.

In May 1840 the firm received an order from the Birmingham & Gloucester Railway for the supply of three locomotive engines:

The above Engines, shall be made like the Sample Engine called 'Victoria' ... Except that a 2nd safety valve shall be made & affixed to the boiler ... in some convenient spot out of the immediate reach of the Engine Men & the scale of each of the valves shall be graduated so as to shew directly in figures the pressure of steam in the boiler per sq. inch and not in triplicate proportion...[32]

A further three engines were ordered during August 1840.

The *Victoria* was manufactured by William Norris (1802-1867) of Philadelphia and Captain

NASMYTH. WILSON & CO. LIMITED

GREAT WESTERN RAILWAY.
7ᴱᵀ GAUGE
16 LOCOMOTIVES & TENDERS TO THE DESIGNS.
OF THE LATE
SIR DANIEL GOOCH..

1841		1842	
ACHILLES	JUNE 1841	ORION	MARCH 1842
MILO	JULY "	DAMON	" "
HECTOR	AUGUST "	ELECTRA	" "
CASTOR	" "	PRIAM	" "
MENTOR	NOV. "	POLLUX	JULY "
BELLONA	DEC. "	PHOENIX	AUG "
ACTAEON	" "	PEGASUS	DEC "
CENTAUR	" "	STENTOR	" "

MAKERS Nᴼˢ 25 - 32

CONSTRUCTED BY

NASMYTH·GASKELL & Cᴼ
AT THE
BRIDGEWATER·FOUNDRY·PATRICROFT..
1841 & 1842.

MAKERS Nᴼˢ 35 - 42

Commemorative board of Great Western Railway contract, 1841-1842. (SLHL)

W.S. Moorsom (1804-1863), chief engineer to the Birmingham & Gloucester Railway, ordered seventeen Norris engines from America so that the Lickey incline, a two-and-a-half-mile slope of 1 in 37, could be worked by locomotives. Nine Norris-pattern engines were subsequently ordered from English firms, three from Benjamin Hick & Son of Bolton and six from Nasmyths Gaskell & Co. Both the Stephenson and Bury firms declined building engines similar to the *Victoria*.

It appears that Nasmyth's sole working guide to the construction of the Norris engines was his inspection of the sample locomotive, for in December 1840 his firm wrote to the railway company in reply to a complaint from Captain Moorsom that the firm had made departures from the specification. Nasmyths Gaskell & Co. noted that they had not received a specification as such and that the only departures made from the sample engine were evident improvements.[33] These comprised substituting wrought-iron and brass for cast-iron 'in many instances where the latter material is not safe' together with alterations to the cross heads of the pistons.[34] The first three locomotives delivered to the railway, *Defford*, *Ashchurch* and *Droitwich*, were fitted with iron fireboxes and extras such as 'Copper Dome and wooden clothing round firebox £11' and 'Bumping apparatus in front of engine £9' making the total price with tender, which cost £185, up to £1,255. The second batch of locomotives delivered during the summer of 1841 were more expensive as an additional £70 was charged for copper fireboxes.[35]

In November 1841 two Norris engines, *Cyclop* and *Goliath*, were shipped by Messrs Zwilchenbart of Liverpool to the Kaiser Ferdinand-Nordbahn of Austria. These were the Bridgewater Foundry's first locomotive export sales and the engines were invoiced at £1,250 each, together with £50 for spare driving wheels, £70 for 'extra thickness of copper for firebox plates' and £25 packing charge.[36] Few could have foreseen at this stage that the export locomotive markets would provide the foundation for the firm's later reputation and commercial prosperity.

The most remunerative order received by Nasmyths Gaskell & Co. during the first phase of locomotive construction was for twenty engines and tenders placed by the Great Western Railway in August 1840. This contract accounted for more than £50,000 of sales. The engines were built in batches of four according to the drawings and specifications supplied by Daniel Gooch (1816-1889), the company's locomotive superintendent.[37] The design was modified in certain respects as the order proceeded and surviving invoices show that steel tyres were substituted for wrought-iron tyres on both engines and tenders at an additional cost of £74 and £56 respectively. A more important alteration was the conversion of the last four engines, *Hercules, Samson, Goliath* and *Tityos*, from 2-2-2 passenger engines to goods engines of the 0-6-0 type. These four locomotives, delivered during the summer and autumn of 1842, had outside sandwich frames and outside bearings and were the only six-coupled engines built with these features for the Great Western broad gauge, all succeeding goods locomotives being designed with the frames inside the wheels. As a further peculiarity, they were noteworthy for being the only six-coupled broad gauge engines built for the railway by an outside firm, all their successors being produced at the company's Swindon Works.[38] The sixteen passenger engines were delivered between June 1841 and December 1842. *Actaeon* was used for the opening of the Bristol and Exeter line on 1 May 1844 and Daniel Gooch drove the engine himself from Paddington to Exeter and back, a distance of 388 miles, with a load of 50 tons. She blew up a few years later and was rebuilt in August 1856. *Orion* was subsequently converted into an eight-wheeled saddle-tank engine and *Castor* was rebuilt in September 1865.[39]

The contract price for the sixteen 2-2-2 engines was £1,800 with the company paying an additional £100 per engine after they had completed successfully a month's trial on the line.[40] Nasmyth claimed that the company also supplied a spontaneous testimonial as to the excellence of the manufacturer's workmanship. While there is no reason to suppose that the company was dissatisfied with their locomotives, their testimonial was not so unprompted as Nasmyth later maintained:

Might I beg you as a most valued favor that you would favor us with a few lines expressive of your opinion as to the performance of the engines … I need not say how truly valuable and important to us would be a few words coming from so high an authority as yourself…[41]

Brunel's confidential opinion of the respective merits of the various locomotive manufacturers with whom he had had dealings is revealed in a letter to Maudslay's written shortly after he had received the 2-2-2 passenger engines:

Fenton Murray & Co. have turned out the <u>best</u> work decidedly – their workmanship is perfect. Stephenson of course is very good – both of these makers get high prices. Hawthorns turn out good work at moderate prices – Nasmyth Gaskell of Manchester and Stothert of Bristol have made excellent engines for us and at low prices – but they <u>all</u> require close looking after …[42]

The Great Western contract was a welcome stimulus to Nasmyths Gaskell & Co. who were still in their early years. But the very size of the order appears to have posed the problem of providing enough cash to pay for the various raw materials and bought-in finished parts. With two-thirds of the sales price payable on delivery and the remaining third after the completion of 3,000 miles, a considerable strain was placed on the financial resources of the firm which was obliged to seek 'a remittance on account'.[43] These problems of cash flow were of minor significance, however, when set beside the benefits that accrued from the contract. This single order was largely responsible for averting some of the worst effects of the current trade depression and as sales of machine tools and steam engines declined during 1841 and 1842, revenue from the Great Western Railway increased such that in the former year they comprised thirty-eight per cent of turnover rising to seventy-one per cent during the following year. While the firm's profits were almost certainly quite slim, it was able to maintain the labour force and extend its reputation at a time when many engineering businesses were facing bankruptcy and closure.

During the second phase of locomotive construction at the Bridgewater Foundry, 1845-1853, sixty-three engines left the works at a total sales value of over £139,000 with the purchasers comprising Robert Stephenson & Co., the York, Newcastle & Berwick Railway, the London & North Western Railway and the Great Northern Railway. The first four years of this phase spanned the 'railway mania', an attempt to complete the railway system in a 'single final bound' when Parliament authorized some 671 Railway Acts and gave its authority for raising £247 million of capital intended for over 11,000 miles of line.[44] With more than five years' experience of meeting the locomotive requirements of the major railway companies, Nasmyth Gaskell & Co. were well placed to stake their claim for a significant share of the new business and achieved sales valued at over £80,000 during the 'mania'.

Few of the firm's detailed records have survived in connection with these contracts with

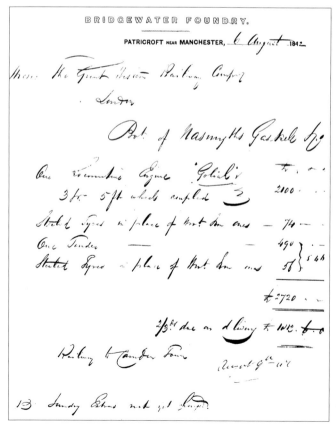

Invoice for NW 45 of 1842 for the Great Western Railway. (SLHL)

the exception of the order and sales books. It appears that sometime during the later half of 1844, Nasmyth Gaskell & Co. made an arrangement with Robert Stephenson & Co. to build locomotives to their instructions and between October 1845 and November 1847, twenty-seven engines and twenty-five tenders were invoiced to Stephenson's Newcastle Works. Fifteen of the twenty-seven locomotives were dispatched to the South Eastern Railway, where thirteen of the engines were used on the Dover line. All fifteen locomotives were of the Stephenson 'long boiler' type and two order book entries for January and March 1845 show that Nasmyth made some minor modifications to Stephenson's design:

Mr Robt Stephenson says he has no objection to the alterations proposed in Mr JN's letter of 22nd Jany. R. Stephenson & Co. per Edwd F Starbuck, Agree to Mr JN's plan for the construction of the bottom of the Fire Boxes.[45]

Two of the Stephenson locomotives were delivered to the Paris & Orleans Railway, bringing the total number of exported Nasmyth engines to four. Great care was taken with the delivery of these machines and a mechanic was sent to Liverpool to superintend shipment. A charge of £15 per engine is recorded for 'eleven packing cases and packing... bright parts in flannel & carefully tallowed'.[46] Of the remaining ten Stephenson engines, eight were delivered to the recently amalgamated London & North Western Railway, which brought together the Grand Junction, London & Birmingham and Manchester & Birmingham Railway companies. The engines had originally been ordered by the London & Birmingham Railway in February 1845. The final two engines, and accompanying six-wheeled tenders, were received by another important amalgamation, the York, Newcastle & Berwick Railway.

The London & North Western Railway was obviously pleased with the Nasmyth engines it had received via Stephenson and directly ordered another six locomotives, delivered during the winter of 1847/1848, to work the mineral traffic on the Southern Division. Similarly, the York, Newcastle & Berwick Railway placed an order for twenty 'long boiler' engines priced at £2,550 for each locomotive and tender. A memorandum of alterations, dated 2 July 1847, reveals a number of interesting points of detail:

The Engines are generally similar to the Goods Engines now being made by N. G. & Co. on Messrs Robert Stephenson & Co.'s patent principle for the London & North Western Railway Co, but to be altered as follows – viz. Tubes to be of Brass instead of Iron, say 117 Brass Tubes 2in diar. Mud hole & plug in each side of blast pipe. Boiler to be clothed with sheet Iron ... Elliptical springs to Tender. Middle axle boxes to be made stronger. Plug hole on each side of outside fire box one-and-a-quarter in diar to correspond with roof of inside fire box ...[47]

The consideration for these alterations was £100 per engine. Delivery of the locomotives was made in batches of two between June 1848 and June 1851. As with the Great Western order the contract with the York, Newcastle & Berwick Railway made an important contribution to the trade of the Bridgewater Foundry when orders for other engineering goods were depressed during 1849 and 1850. Locomotive revenues during these two years constituted more than forty per cent of turnover.

Nasmyth's final locomotive contract was for the supply of ten goods engines to be built to the designs of Archibald Sturrock (1816-1909) for the Great Northern Railway. The name of Nasmyth Gaskell & Co. must have been familiar to Sturrock as he had previously worked for William Fairbairn in Manchester and Daniel Gooch at the Great Western Railway.[48] The invoice price for locomotive and tender together was £2,220 and the firm received £22,200 for the ten deliveries.

Although less than seven per cent of the Bridgewater Foundry's total locomotive output was achieved under Nasmyth, he must be given the credit for establishing and consolidating the firm's locomotive-building business. This was achieved by offering competitive prices to the railway companies and by producing high quality workmanship. It may also have owed something to the various design improvements offered by James Nasmyth two of which were patented and offered to prospective locomotive purchasers.[49] Yet at this time the Bridgewater Foundry was one of the smaller locomotive manufacturers both in regional and national terms. The firm's average output between 1838 and 1853 was 7.3 engines. Only the Haigh Foundry with an average for the same period of 5.5 engines had a lower output among the main regional competitors. Sharp Stewart, latterly Sharp Roberts & Co. of Manchester had an average output of fifty and this exceeded the output of the country's most famous and long-established locomotive manufacturer, Robert Stephenson & Co., by two engines per year. Yet the role of locomotive manufacture at the Bridgewater Foundry was such as to protect the firm from the worst effects of the depressions for general engineering goods. For while the railway companies placed their orders in times of buoyant trade, by the time the orders came to be paid for the commercial conditions were often very different. This helped to even out the fluctuations of the firm's trade cycle. Had Nasmyth devoted more of his production activities to locomotive manufacture he would have had to have coped with market conditions that could change quite dramatically between one year and the next – the total number of locomotives produced nationwide in 1849 was estimated at 398 compared to 197 during the following year, for example.[50] By maintaining a broad product range, with differing trading characteristics, he was able to steer the firm through those hard times that during the 1850s had claimed, in the North West alone, the scalps of Edward Bury's business, Jones & Potts of Newton-Le-Willows and the Haigh Foundry.

NW 37 of 1842 for Great Western Railway. One of the earliest surviving photographs of a Nasmyth locomotive. (SLHL)

six
The Wilson Years
1857-1882

Robert Wilson, the Wilson of Nasmyth Wilson, took over from James Nasmyth as managing partner at the Bridgewater Foundry from the beginning of 1857 and remained in that position until shortly before his death in July 1882. A new partnership agreement, dated January 1857, was drawn up which added Henry Garnett's sons, Charles Henry (1842-1917) and Robert (1845-1921), to the firm. In October 1867, the Garnett brothers withdrew from the business leaving Robert Wilson and Henry Garnett in joint control. Henry Garnett left the firm in January 1877 to be replaced by his son Stewart (1850-1921) and Robert Wilson junior (1851-1898). It appears that deteriorating relations between Wilson senior and Henry Garnett had been the primary reason for the latter's retirement. In a letter to Nasmyth dated January 1877, Garnett complained of Wilson's 'unsatisfactory conduct … whose behaviour to me since the last ten years has been anything but agreeable'.[1] The causes of the friction remain unknown but may have related to the building extensions of the mid-to-late 1860s which must have involved a substantial capital outlay and some considerable risk.[2]

Robert Wilson had previously served as works manager at the Bridgewater Foundry between approximately 1840 and 1845. Born in Dunbar, a small seaport on the east coast of Scotland, in September 1803, he enjoyed none of Nasmyth's advantages of background and education. His father, Benjamin Wilson, a cooper-cum-mariner,[3] was drowned at sea in December 1810 while engaged in a rescue attempt to save the crew of the *Pallas* which was wrecked on the Vault Shore.[4] Robert Wilson had to depend on his mother for much of his upbringing and later paid tribute to the way she had extolled 'the evils of dishonesty, and the great rewards of truth and integrity of purpose'. Wilson claimed that he had worked from the age of nine and had 'never worn a pair of shoes but what he had paid for out of his own earnings'. Wilson was a dedicated exponent of 'self-application', 'self-education', 'steadiness and perseverance'. In order to compensate for the lack of a 'sound education' he had, in early manhood, employed a private tutor and paid him at the rate of five shillings an hour. He later calculated that he had paid out £34 for being taught.[5] Although apprenticed to a joiner and cabinet-maker, Wilson developed an early interest in mechanics, especially in regard to the screw propulsion of ships. He claimed to have invented the screw propeller for which he was awarded a silver medal in 1832 by the Scottish Society of Arts. The design was laid before the Admiralty in 1827 and 1833, who rejected it on both occasions, only to adopt it at a later date, under a different sponsor, following Francis Pettit Smith's patent of May 1836.

It was in 1828, while making experiments with a model of his screw-propeller at Leith, that Wilson first met James Nasmyth who was then building his road steam carriage. Apparently, Nasmyth formed a favourable opinion of Wilson's mechanical knowledge when the latter pointed out 'a great mechanical error' in the construction of the steam carriage engines.[6] During the early 1830s Wilson was working as an engineer in Edinburgh, at an address in North Back of Canongate,[7] where he almost certainly re-established contact with the Nasmyths. Precisely when Wilson moved south to Patricroft is unclear.[8] Family events suggest that he was still in

Edinburgh in 1839[9] and Wilson himself claimed, in 1874, that he had moved to Patricroft in 1840.[10] His principal achievement while employed as works manager was to devise the self-acting mechanism that was to convert the steam hammer into a workable and therefore commercial proposition. That was to cause future ructions between himself and Nasmyth for when the latter published the first account of the steam hammer in 1863[11] no mention was made of Wilson's contribution. Up to that point relations between the two men appear to have been reasonably cordial and Wilson named a son born in 1856 James Nasmyth Wilson. But Wilson was incensed by the snub and set about putting the record straight by arranging for a public lecture followed by a published pamphlet to set forth the true facts of the matter.[12] Wilson's case was supported by Holbrook Gaskell, the chief cashier who delivered the lecture, the former foreman of the smiths and others. This, in turn, infuriated Nasmyth who omitted all mention of Wilson in his *Autobiography* and took every occasion to blacken Wilson's name in his correspondence with Samuel Smiles. On hearing of his former employee's death Nasmyth wrote to Smiles, 'Wilson is Dead at the age of 79 he was an able man in many ways in connection with machinery but so eaten up with self conceit and damaged by a treacherous disposition as to render him far from a desirable associate or one to have business dealings with – but he is gone so there is an end to his doings good bad and indifferent'.[13] On another occasion Nasmyth commented that Wilson's 'attempt to claim the screw propeller as his invention is all of a piece with his systematic grasping conceit' and referred to Wilson and his supporters as 'wasps and mosquitos'.[14] Nasmyth's obsession with protecting his reputation as the inventor of the steam hammer, even to the extent that he incorporated the machine into his family coat of arms, and

Left and opposite: *Three machine tools manufactured during the Wilson years:*

Left: *Drilling machine* (left).

Opposite above: *Wheel-turning lathe*

Opposite below: *Planing machine, (SLHL).*

his refusal to publically refute Wilson's claim on the grounds that the 'best way to meet such detractors is silence', in stark contrast to the way he dealt with the counter claims of a French engineer,[15] all suggest that Wilson had hit a very raw nerve.

During the mid-1840s Wilson crossed the Pennines to take up employment as works manager at the Low Moor Ironworks, near Bradford. He returned to Patricroft as working partner designate in July 1856. During the twenty-five years that Wilson was in charge the firm slowly changed from a general engineering business to one that specialized in the building of locomotives. The specialization was never complete, however, and the firm continued accepting orders for a wide variety of engineering goods. The steam hammer and pile driver, for example, remained staple products with 388 of these machines manufactured between 1857 and 1882, the most valuable order being a 30-ton hammer and accompanying forge cranes for the Royal Arsenal, Woolwich, delivered in 1873. Steam engines and boilers also remained in regular demand[16] and an article on the Bridgewater Foundry, dated 1867, refers to the 'largest engines ever made at Patricroft now under construction for the Kirkless Hall Co., at Wigan'. These were blowing engines with 100in diameter blowing cylinders, a stroke of 12ft, and a 30ft beam weighing 32 tons.[17]

The most important new product line was that of the hydraulic press. This reflected Wilson's interest in hydraulic machinery for which he took out eleven patents. The first of these, dated 1856, was in conjunction with Nasmyth[18] but he soon branched out on his own. Wilson's hydraulic presses were designed for packing cotton, flax, hemp and jute and had particular application on the Indian sub-continent and in Egypt. One invention of 1875 comprised a horizontal hydraulic packing press.[19] A sales description claimed that it 'is particularly suitable for up-country packing establishments, as it can be placed on the floor of a shed, requires no foundation, and entirely dispenses with the lofty and expensive buildings hitherto required'.[20] Another invention, the compound baling and finishing press, patented in 1876, was intended to replace the ordinary press and auxiliary finisher thereby saving both time and expense in pressing the bale.[21] During the Wilson years 182 presses[22] were manufactured at Patricroft, an average of more than seven per year. Since a press could sell for more than £1,400 and orders were often accompanied by requests for steam engines and boilers, this new line of business made a significant contribution to turnover. In 1873 Wilson sent his son Robert to India for two years to superintend the erection of machinery and establish agencies for the firm in the cotton-pressing centres. Even before that visit there are references in the sales records to a Nasmyth Press Co., Ltd of Calcutta.[23]

Much of the day-to-day running of the Bridgewater Foundry would have been in the hands of the various works managers. It is not possible to establish a completely continuous list between 1857 and 1882 but records show that Thomas Crewdson, a former foreman of the smiths, served in this capacity between 1860 and 1861 followed by John Nuttall (1818-1890)[24] who retired in 1872 and then John Henry Davis (1837-1896)[25] who left Patricroft to become a London-based consulting engineer in 1877. It is possible that between 1877 and 1882 the job was effectively performed by Robert Wilson junior for in the former year he had become a partner in the firm. Both Nuttall and Davis were well qualified for senior positions in a locomotive-building firm. Nuttall had previously worked for three other leading locomotive builders in the north west – Jones, Turner & Evans, where he served his apprenticeship, Sharp, Roberts & Co., where he was foreman smith and then Beyer, Peacock & Co. where he introduced his improvements to the tuyère and smith's hearth. At Patricroft, Nuttall was a co-patentee with Wilson senior of a new method for forging axles, the patentee of a valve and the improver of a new turning tool. Davis served his apprenticeship at the Crewe workshops of the London & North Western Railway followed by twelve months in the locomotive department of the London & South Western Railway. He then worked in the drawing office of Neilson & Co. of Glasgow and the design department of Sharp, Stewart & Co. Such experience in charge of the shop floor meant that Wilson senior had opportunities to indulge his inventive faculties. He took out twenty-four patents during his years at the helm.[26]

Although, by 1882, Nasmyth Wilson had become a specialist locomotive manufacturer, the future direction of the firm did not become apparent until the 1870s. Only ten locomotives were built during the first fifteen years of Wilson's stewardship, all of them for the domestic market. During the following decade ninety-six locomotives left the works, only eight of which were for British customers. Not only did the firm become increasingly drawn into locomotive manufacture but the trade became increasingly dominated by the export market. That was to remain a prime feature of the firm's business. Another emerging trend concerned the variety of gauges. All the locomotives manufactured under Nasmyth were for the standard gauge apart from the twenty 7ft gauge engines built for the Great Western. Wilson built locomotives to six different gauges, the most popular being the forty-six engines for the Indian State Railway which employed the metre gauge.

During Wilson's first four years in charge, no locomotives were built at Patricroft. In 1861 and 1862 four engines were delivered to the Kirkless Hall Coal & Iron Co. near Wigan where Wilson's brother-in-law, John Lancaster, was the proprietor.[27] There was then a four-year break until 1867 when six 2-2-2 engines were made for the London, Brighton & South Coast Railway. Another four-year break occurred before the next consignment of five 0-6-0 engines and tenders for the Great Eastern Railway in 1872.[28] The following year marked the beginning of the lucrative connection with India when seventeen 0-4-4 tank engines[29] were sent to the Indian State Railway. There are no surviving records as to how the Indian trade was developed, but it cannot have been an accident that Nasmyth Wilson was already involved in substantial business with the subcontinent in relation to the supply of hydraulic cotton-packing presses and other engineering equipment. The Indian raw cotton trade and the building of railways were closely linked and the construction of the Indian railway network came about, in part, from pressure exerted on the East India Co. by representatives of the Lancashire cotton industry who wanted an alternative source of supply to the United States. The Indian railways which began in 1850 and amounted to nearly 10,000 miles of track by 1881, made it possible to expand the cotton and jute growing areas by linking the hinterland with the ports of Bombay and Calcutta. That would have stimulated the demand for cotton presses which continued to be a staple product at the Bridgewater Foundry until the late 1930s. Hence, as far as India was concerned, the trade in locomotives and packing presses was mutually reinforcing.

The three principal export destinations after India were Spain (twenty engines), Chile (eight engines) and Sweden (seven engines). Eleven of the Spanish engines were purchased by the Majorca Railway Co. which was originally formed in 1872 to provide an eighteen-mile railway connection between the capital, Palma, and Inca. Nasmyth Wilson provided the Majorca railways with all their imported locomotives until the First World War ended the connection, the first three engines appropriately named *Mallorca*, *Palma* and *Inca*.[30] The remaining nine engines for Spain, six 0-6-0s and three 2-4-0s, were for the broad-gauge Almansa Valencia Railway. The eight 0-6-0 tank engines sent to Chile were for the Tal Tal Railway while the seven 0-6-0 engines, six tank and one saddle tank, for Sweden were to run on the Nora Kariskoga Railway. The remaining exports, two 0-6-0 tank engines, were delivered to the Mount Keira Colliery in New South Wales to connect the coal mine with the wharf at Belmore Basin.

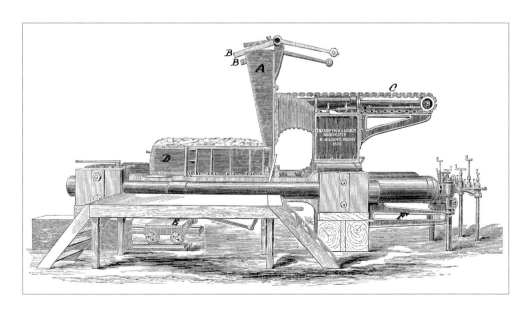

Wilson's patent horizontal hydraulic cotton-packing press, 1875. (SLHL)

By 1882 Nasmyth Wilson was one of the nation's principal and most well-established locomotive manufacturers. Of the fourteen firms established before 1845 that produced more than 100 locomotives, half had ceased production by 1865 including E.B. Wilson & Co. of Leeds and R.B. Longridge & Co. of Bedlington.[31] Nasmyth's had survived and seen off the competition but though the firm was clearly one of the major builders in the industry it was not one of the giants. Even within the North West, Nasmyth's took fourth place in terms of locomotive output after Beyer Peacock, Sharp Stewart and The Vulcan Foundry. The maximum annual locomotive output of the Bridgewater Foundry by the end of 1881 was thirty-two engines compared with 123 for Beyer Peacock.[32] In the early 1880s, Nasmyth Wilson was the ninth largest private locomotive builder in terms of output, but although the firm majored in locomotive manufacture it was not as specialist as the more recently established firms such as Beyer Peacock (1855) and Dubs (1865).

In contrast to his former employer, James Nasmyth, who enjoyed a retirement of more than thirty years at Penshurst in Kent, Robert Wilson remained a working engineer until the end of his life. While Nasmyth was busy preparing his memoirs for publication, Wilson was still inventing and his last patent for vertical steam engines was dated September 1880.[33] In the same year the War Office granted Wilson £500 for the use of his double-action screw propeller as applied to the fish torpedo. One of the last contributions Wilson made to his firm was to oversee its transition to a limited company in May 1882. Between this date and his death at Matlock on 28 July, Robert Wilson was Chairman of Nasmyth Wilson & Co. Ltd. Unlike Nasmyth who was both loquacious and egotistical, Wilson appears to have been both quiet and unassuming except when roused to

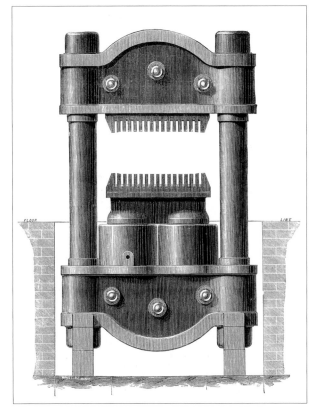

Wilson's patent finishing press, 1876. (SLHL)

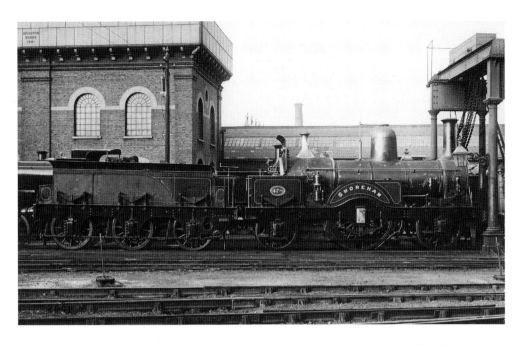

NW 116 of 1867 for the London, Brighton & South Coast Railway. (L.G. Marshall Collection)

self-justification by having his achievements either belittled or ignored. One anecdotal recollection describes him as 'an ingenious man, but a man of few words' while another calls him a 'shrewd and genial Scotsman'.[34] In his obituary notice on Robert Wilson for the Proceedings of the Royal Society of Edinburgh, the electrical engineer and scientist, Fleeming Jenkin, concluded with the following words:

Mr Wilson will be remembered as worthy of mention among the group of able Scotch mechanicians who, by their power of invention, energy, and business capacity, have not only won distinction and wealth for themselves, but have added to the resources and strength of the empire.[35]

NW 124 of 1872 for the Great Eastern Railway. (SLHL)

NW 148 of 1874 for the Indian State Railway. Picture printed in reverse. (SLHL)

NW 174 of 1874 for the Majorca Railway. (SLHL)

NW 183 of 1875 for North West Provinces, Indian State Railway. (SLHL)

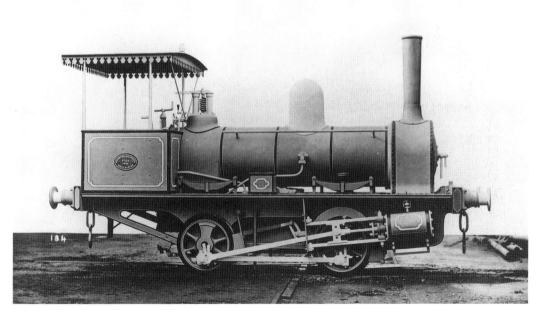

NW 184 of 1875 for Manchester Corporation Gas Works. (SLHL)

NW 188 of 1876 for the Majorca Railway at Palma, 1957. (L.G. Marshall)

NW 189 of 1876 for the Majorca Railway at Palma, 1957. (L.G. Marshall)

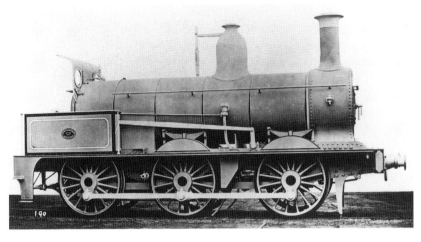

NW 190 of 1876 for the Valencia Railway. (SLHL)

NW 199 of 1878 for Mount Keira Colliery, New South Wales. (SLHL)

NW 200 of 1878 for the Valencia Railway at Valencia, 1953. (D. Trevor Rowe)

seven
Nasmyth, Wilson & Co. Ltd
1882-1919

When Nasmyth Wilson & Co. became a limited company in May 1882 the intention of the directors was to retain all the essential features of a family firm but with the additional security provided by limited liability. That was a prudent move given the increasing trend towards the manufacture of a relatively small number of high value products – locomotives, steam hammers and hydraulic machinery – most of which were destined for the now highly competitive export markets. That competition resulted, in particular, from the industrialization of the German and United States economies both of which overtook the British in terms of steel production during the 1890s.

The first directors of the new company were Henry Garnett, Robert Wilson (chairman), Stewart Garnett and Robert Wilson junior (joint managing directors).[1] The old partnership had been valued at £80,000 and half of that was raised by an ordinary share issue and the other half through the creation of five per cent debenture stock.[2] There were originally eight shareholders owning a total of 525 out of an authorized 1,000 £100 shares with calls of £80 per share. Since five persons held just one share each, control rested with Robert Wilson senior (150 shares), Stewart Garnett (225 shares) and Robert Wilson junior (125 shares).[3] Ten years later 565 shares had been taken up with calls of £100 per £100 share. The number of shareholders had increased to sixteen, six of whom were members of the Garnett or Wilson families (358 shares in total). Other shareholders included John Goodier, the company's cashier and a future director (twenty shares), Thomas Daniels, the works manager and a future director (seven shares) and William Smethurst,[4] engineer and chief draughtsman (five shares).[5] Hence while the firm was legally a public company, the share ownership was essentially confined to directors, senior employees and those with financial or social relations with the business. That position was substantially the same in 1902 with eleven new shareholders added to the register most of whom had identifiable links to the company such as the widows of Robert Wilson junior and Thomas Daniels and the son-in-law and grand-daughter of Robert Wilson senior.[6] Hence, when Nasmyth Wilson converted into a private company in 1908, following the enabling legislation of the previous year, it was simply receiving an appropriate legal status for its ownership structure. A small directorate who owned the majority of the ordinary shares continued to exercise exactly the same form of close control as had formerly been exercised by the firm's partners. Capital resources came from ploughed-back profits and bank loans without recourse to the stock exchange.

During this period the major personalities associated with the company directorate were Robert Wilson junior, Stewart Garnett and Edward Hyde Greg. A number of Robert Wilson senior's sons appear to have been associated with the firm[7] but his eldest son, Robert, played the most important role.[8] Educated at the Edinburgh Academy and Edinburgh University, he gained his practical training in the engineering departments and drawing office of the Bridgewater Foundry. While becoming joint managing director of Nasmyth's in 1882, his principal role must have been that of sales director. By 1875 he had already visited India, Burma, China, Japan and South America and in 1881 and 1883 he made professional visits to Spain and Majorca.

NW 230 of 1883 for Sharp Stewart & Co., probably for Spain. (SLHL)

NW 241 of 1884 for Bahia Railway. Picture printed in reverse. (SLHL)

NW 253 of 1884 for the New Zealand Government Railway. (SLHL)

NW 264 of 1884 for the Santa Fé Railway. (SLHL)

NW 285 of 1884 for the La Guaira & Caracus Railway. (SLHL)

NW 339 of 1888 for Sanyo Railway. (SLHL)

Combining his company duties with work as a consulting engineer in Westminster, he travelled to New Zealand in 1886 where he became one of the consulting engineers to the Government and engineer-in-chief and general manager of the New Zealand Midland Railway. Prior to that he had been joint engineer in England for a number of New Zealand railway concerns together with the Antimano Railway in Venezuela. Wilson's death at the early age of forty-six deprived Nasmyth's of an able and successful overseas representative for his travels and contacts had often led to new orders for locomotives as well as the consolidation of existing business relations.

As with Robert Wilson junior, Stewart Garnett, the sixth son of Henry Garnett, was successively partner (1877) and joint managing director (1882). From around 1900 he became chairman, a position he was to hold for twenty years. Along with his brothers, Charles and Robert, who had been partners in the firm, Stewart was educated at Cheltenham College after which he probably gained practical engineering experience at Nasmyth's. Information on Garnett's contribution to the company is thin but his business acumen was sufficient for him to be invited onto the board of the Lancashire & Yorkshire Railway in 1897.[9] It is possible that he improved the business prospects of the company through his marriage to Caroline Sugden Armitage the only daughter of the cotton spinner Elkanah Armitage. The latter's father of the same name founded the firm of Armitage & Co. of London and Manchester in 1827 and became Manchester's mayor between 1846 and 1848. When Stewart Garnett died on 31 January 1921 the probate value of his estate was assessed at £86,855 13s 5d.[10]

Edward Hyde Greg junior (1864-1946)[11] became managing director of Nasmyth's around the turn of the century[12] and remained in this post until the end of March 1938.[13] His resignation may have been prompted by the end of locomotive production. Quite how he became introduced to

A pre-1906 works nameplate. (SLHL)

NW 414 of 1891 for the Majorca Railway at Palma, 1957. (L.G. Marshall)

NW 428 of 1892 for the London, Tilbury & Southend Railway. (L.G. Marshall Collection)

NW 432 of 1892 for Somorrostro Iron Ore Co. (SLHL)

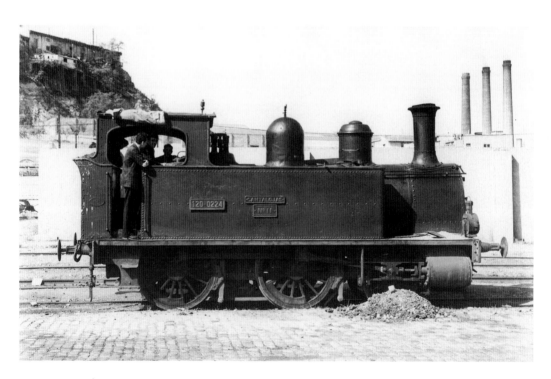

NW 444 of 1893 for the Bilbao & Portugalete Railway at Barcelona, 1957. (L.G. Marshall)

NW 445 of 1893 for Bury Corporation. (SLHL)

NW 462 of 1895 for the Cambrian Railway. (L.G. Marshall Collection)

Nasmyth's is uncertain though there are at least two strong possibilities. Greg was the third son of Edward Hyde Greg (1827-1910) and the great-grandson of Samuel Greg the founder of the famous Quarry Bank spinning mill at Styal, Cheshire. Prominent local cotton manufacturing families were certain to know each other and the Garnetts may have been introduced to the Gregs through Elkanah Armitage. Alternatively, one of the family seats of the Garnett family was based outside Lancaster at Quernmore. Close neighbours with adjoining land was a branch of the Greg family of Escowbeck, Caton. Albert Greg of Escowbeck held forty shares in Nasmyth's in 1902.[14] Perhaps a social relationship led to business opportunity. Edward Hyde Greg junior attended Rugby between 1878 and 1882 and then may have assisted his father with management duties at Styal. Curiously, though resident at Quarry Bank, he is described as a 'Student of Electric Engineering' in the 1891 census. His character must have been formed partly in contrast to his father's extravagance and vanity for as early as 1884 he delivered a stern filial rebuke at the frittering away of much needed moneys on dinner parties and expensive presents.[15] As with Stewart Garnett there is little record of his activities at the Bridgewater Foundry apart from records of his attendance at meetings of the Locomotive Manufacturers' Association and some business correspondence concerning the pricing of locomotive contracts. It would appear that he was a popular and well-regarded manager judging by the wedding gifts he received from his employees in 1910 – these included a handsome silver flower stand from the factory workforce, a silver fruit dish from the general office staff and a combined foot-rest and luncheon basket, specially arranged for a motor car, from the works manager, head draughtsman and head of the London office.[16] Greg combined his duties at Patricroft with a directorship of Quarry Bank Mill Ltd between 1923 and 1939.[17]

NW 554 of 1899 for the Furness Railway. (L.G. Marshall Collection)

NW 593 of 1900 for the North Staffordshire Railway. (R.N. Redman Collection)

There were two long serving works managers at the Bridgewater Foundry during these years. Thomas Daniels (1841-1900)[18] became works manager in 1883 and was succeeded by James Bolas (1860-1937)[19] on his death, by which time he had also served for three years as a director. Daniels arrived at Patricroft with an impressive accumulation of engineering experience having served his apprenticeship in the Wolverton workshop of the London & North Western Railway. He later became foreman of the machine shops at the Worcester Engine Works followed by nine years as foreman of the erecting shops at Sharp, Stewart & Co., Manchester. He obviously acquired a reputation as a conciliator for it was claimed there had never been a single dispute with the workmen during his connection with the firm.[20] James Bolas came to the Bridgewater Foundry at approximately the same time as Daniels following an apprenticeship at Kitson & Co., Leeds where his father worked as a foreman engine smith. After two years at The Vulcan Foundry, Newton-le-Willows, Bolas began work at Patricroft as a draughtsman rising to become chief draughtsman before taking over as works manager in March 1900. In 1911 Bolas patented an improved construction of riveting tool, an invention in which the company purchased an interest during the following year.[21] This was the last patent associated with Nasmyth's for a tool and the invention was used in connection with boiler and fire-box manufacture. Bolas was clearly a highly valued employee of the company and was retained in an advisory capacity when he retired after more than fifty years service.

All contemporary accounts stress the primacy of locomotive production during the period 1882 to 1919. The local newspaper stated in 1907 that locomotive building was 'at present the principal part of the business',[22] while *The Railway Gazette* of 1913 claimed that the company was 'principally identified with the production of locomotive engines of all sizes and types, and for every class of service'. The same journal also conceded that 'a considerable amount of work other than the building of locomotives is carried on, chiefly in connection with heavy hydraulic

NW 594 of 1900 for Wigan Coal & Iron Co. (SLHL)

NW 654 of 1902 for Western Australia Government Railway. (SLHL)

NW 680 of 1903 for Delta Railways, Egypt. (SLHL)

NW 710 of 1904 for the Cyprus Government Railway. (SLHL)

machinery and baling presses'.[23] An account of the business dated 1887 gives an interesting insight into the extent that Nasmyth's was then still a general engineering concern specializing in locomotive manufacture:

The capacity of the works generally is equal to a locomotive per week, three or four steam-hammers per week, a pair of hydraulic engines every three weeks, one press about each fortnight, besides a number of other machines and stationary engines, all of which put together makes a not unsatisfactory total of about 3,000 tons of finished work per annum.[24]

The figures quoted here have to be regarded as on the optimistic side since annual production of locomotives only once reached the capacity figure before 1919 and that was in 1917 as a result of a Ministry of Munitions order. A total of 472 steam hammers were manufactured between March 1882 and August 1919, an average of more than one per month.[25] There are no comparable figures for hydraulic presses though James Bolas claimed, when he retired in 1934, that he had been responsible for 704 hydraulic and steam cotton-baling presses since 1900.[26] That would give an average of over twenty a year though there are reasons to suppose that the production would have been greater during the early years of the new century given the depression of the Lancashire textile industry between the wars and the development of India's and Egypt's own textile industries after 1914. One special order completed in 1907 and destined for Egypt was for reputedly the largest cotton press then in existence weighing 150 tons and measuring about 80ft in height which could pack seventy bales of cotton, each weighing 740 lbs. in an hour.[27]

But, while steam hammers and baling presses were useful, subsidiary product lines providing much valued custom when locomotive orders were thin on the ground, it was to the locomotive markets that the main productive and marketing energies of the company were directed during that period. By the beginning of 1882 only 215 locomotives had been delivered to customers during the first forty-four years of trading. That represented an average of less than five engines per year and less than fourteen per cent of the total for the century of locomotive production. Between 1882 and 1919, 1,048 locomotives were dispatched from the works, an average of twenty-eight per year[28] and sixty-four per cent of the total. The export market predominated – accounting for seventy-nine per cent of deliveries – and the figure would have been even

Post-1906 works nameplate. (Ian Manson)

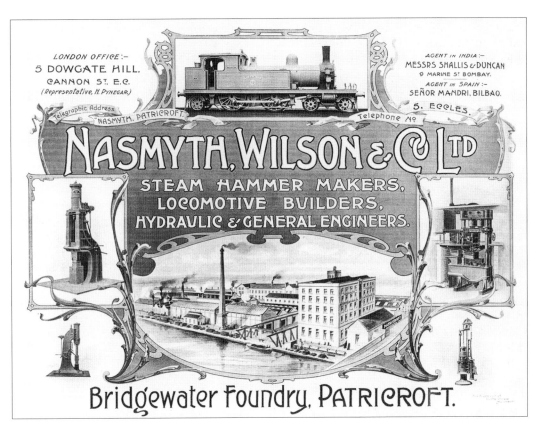

Early twentieth-century advertisement. (SLHL)

greater but for the wartime orders placed by the British Government. If the latter are excluded then exports accounted for over ninety per cent of deliveries. The principal export market was India followed by Japan. Together they accounted for forty-five per cent of total orders.

With the railway company workshops now providing most of the rolling stock for the main line railways[29] the scope for domestic orders was limited. Excluding British Government wartime orders, eighty locomotives were delivered to domestic customers. Much of the business came from the smaller railway companies and industrial undertakings. Many of the latter were local concerns, such as the Wigan Coal & Iron Company and the Earl of Ellesmere's Colliery at Walkden. Both of these enterprises received four 0-6-0 saddle-tank engines.[30] The principal order from a mainland railway company was from the Furness Railway for six 0-6-0s in 1899 and five 0-6-2 tank engines in 1904. That railway was central to the development of Barrow-in-Furness and the expanding coal, iron and slate quarrying industries of West Cumberland. Nasmyth's also assisted in the development of the South Wales coal industry supplying a total of seventeen locomotives to the Neath & Brecon, Brecon & Merthyr and Taff Vale Railways.[31] Six 4-4-2 tank engines were delivered to Plaistow for the London, Tilbury & Southend Railway in 1892, perhaps to help meet the demand provided by the expanding east London suburbs, and six 0-4-4 tank engines were delivered to Oswestry for the Cambrian Railway between 1895 and 1899. Six 0-6-0 engines also went to the North Staffordshire Railway in 1900. Ireland received nineteen locomotives built to three different gauges.[32]

NW 753 of 1906 for Corporation of Western Egypt. (R.N. Redman Collection)

The locomotive specification book kept at Salford Archive Centre contains occasional information both as to the pricing and profitability of the various customer contracts. The first domestic contract for which there is a recorded profit or loss margin was for the 4-4-0 tank engine sent to the West Carberry Railway for £1,100. The firm sustained a loss of twenty-seven-and-a-half per cent. More serious would have been the thirty-three per cent loss on the contract worth £11,988 made with the London, Tilbury & Southend Railway. Four of the nine domestic contracts during the 1890s made a loss, whereas all of the ten contracts negotiated during the 1900s made a profit. That was clearly a good decade for Nasmyth's as in seven of the ten contracts the profit margin was equal to or exceeded fifteen per cent. The lowest profit margin was seven-and-a-quarter per cent on a contract worth £12,214 negotiated with the Furness Railway. It would appear that the company was becoming more adept in its pricing policy and perhaps improving its control over production costs, though the early 1900s were undoubtedly the highpoint for the industry with commercial production achieving a national maximum of 1,300 locomotives in 1907. After 1910, market conditions deteriorated. Out of the seven domestic contracts there is no information on two and of the remaining five the company made a loss in two cases.[33]

Locomotive exports were the bread and butter of the company's business and 836 engines were sent abroad during this period. Between 1882 and 1889, exports amounted to 155 locomotives, an average of nineteen per year, with Central and South America, Japan and Australasia constituting the principal markets. Twenty-one foreign and colonial railways made purchases during the 1880s with the major buyers comprising the Imperial Railways of Japan (thirty-two locomotives), the New Zealand Government (twenty locomotives) and the Queensland Government Railway (fifteen locomotives). Profit and loss data are available from 1887 and these confirm the position suggested by the domestic contract information that the

NW 781 of 1906 for the Trinidad Government Railway. (SLHL)

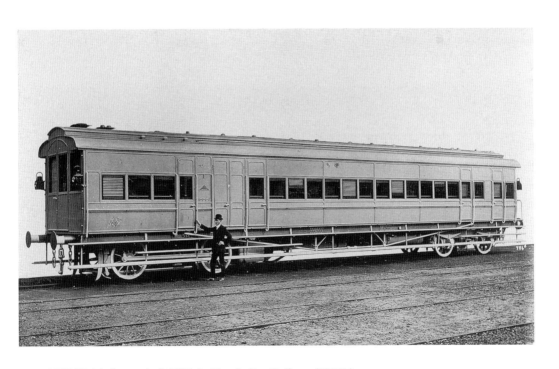

NW 794 (rail motor) of 1907 for East Indian Railway. (SLHL)

NW 803 of 1907 for the Buenos Ayres Great Southern Railway. (R.N. Redman Collection)

NW 828 of 1907 for the County Donegal Railway. (R.N. Redman Collection)

NW 830 of 1908 for the County Donegal Railway. (P. Ransome Wallis Collection, National Railway Museum)

company was experiencing considerable technical/financial problems during these years. Only one contract between 1887 and 1889 resulted in a profit – four export locomotives out of forty-eight. The two 2-6-2 tank engines delivered to the Imperial Railways of Japan in 1888 resulted in a loss of forty-nine per cent while the fifteen 4-6-0 engines sent to the Queensland Government Railway resulted in a twenty per cent loss. One reason for this is provided by the specification book: all the loss-making contracts have the word 'new' recorded against a space for 'Remarks' at the top-right hand side of every page; in the case of the Sorocabana Companhia Railway contract that resulted in a profit of fourteen per cent the words 'same as 250/1' (referring to a previous works number) are recorded. In other words the latter order was a repeat order and the company could learn from past mistakes or problems. Sometimes the problems were not immediately resolved, for while the contract with the Imperial Railways of Japan for ten 2-4-2 tank engines resulted in a eleven-and-a-half per cent loss in 1887/1888 a repeat order for six 2-4-2 tank engines delivered in 1888 resulted in a twelve-and-a-half per cent loss. Nevertheless, when a second repeat for six engines occurred in 1890 a modest profit of two-and-a-half per cent was made. The general rule seems to have been that new designs were more likely to result in losses than profits during the 1880s and early 1890s. This is hardly surprising given that the company was producing for four different gauges for the export market and fourteen different combinations of cylinder size.[34]

LOCOMOTIVES

FOR ALL GAUGES AND ALL CLASSES OF TRAFFIC.

DUPLICATE BOILERS.

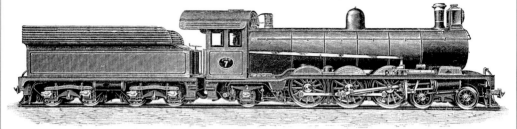

NASMYTH, WILSON & CO., LIMITED,

TELEGRAMS—
NASMYTH, PATRICROFT.

PATRICROFT, Nr. MANCHESTER.

Advertisement featuring NW 833 of 1908 for Johore State Railway. (Railway Yearbook, 1908)

During the 1890s, 167 locomotives were exported, an average of seventeen per year. Japan was the predominant market accounting for over fifty-six per cent of sales with Europe and Central and South America providing sixteen and ten per cent respectively. Orders were received from forty railways with Japanese companies accounting for twenty-three of that number. The pattern of contracts was different from the previous period with only one company, Imperial Railways of Japan, ordering more than twenty locomotives and thirty-one of the customers ordering five locomotives or fewer. It was during the 1890s that Nasmyth's resolved their problems over unprofitable contracts. There is profit/loss data on all but three of the 167 exported locomotives. Up to 1895, thirty-six engines were sold at a loss and thirty-two at a profit. Between 1896 and 1899 nine engines were sold at a loss and eighty-seven at a profit. Furthermore, no engine was sold at a loss between 1897 and 1899. That was partly because many of the locomotives built were the same as or similar to previous locomotives built by the company but even with new designs good profits were now achievable as with the twenty-one-and-a-half per cent profit on the five 0-6-0 tank engines supplied to the Hokuyetsu Railway, Japan in 1898.

The first decade of the twentieth century represented the golden age of locomotive production at the Bridgewater Foundry reflecting the position of the industry as a whole.[35] Total exports amounted to 309 locomotives, an average of thirty-one per year. With Japan beginning her own production in 1892 the importance of this market declined to thirteen per cent of the total, but the Japanese market was still next in importance to India and Burma which accounted for nearly fifty-seven per cent of export sales. The pattern of sales shifted again towards a smaller number of customers who were sometimes prepared to place multiple orders. That would have enabled Nasmyth's to engage in a greater level of batch production. For example, Western Australian Railways received fifteen 4-4-4 tank engines in 1901 and a further fifteen 4-6-2 engines in the following year. Not surprisingly there were good profits of seventeen per cent and eight-and-a-half per cent made on the two consignments respectively. Of the thirty-four railways and

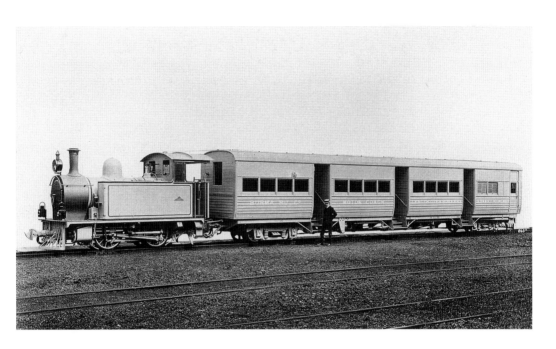

NW 843 (rail motor) of 1908 for Burma Railways. (SLHL)

NW 853 of 1908 for Silla a Cullera Railway. (SLHL)

NW 867 of 1908 for the Assam Bengal Railway. (SLHL)

NW 883 of 1909 for the Southern Nigerian Railway. (SLHL)

NW 890 of 1909 for the Madras & Southern Mahratta Railway. (SLHL)

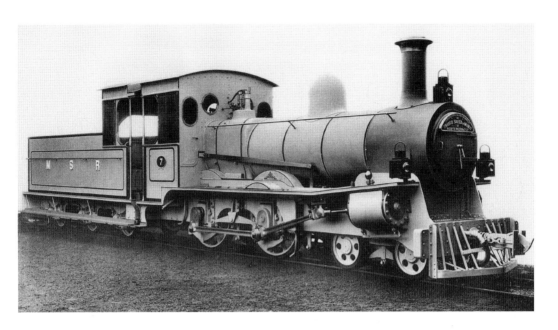

NW 907 of 1909 for Morvi State Railway. (SLHL)

contractors who placed orders during that decade, eleven ordered ten engines or more. The Eastern Bengal Railway received sixty-one locomotives in five major consignments the most important of which was a batch of eighteen 4-6-0 engines delivered in 1907. The profit on that contract priced at £47,862 was thirteen-and-three-quarter per cent. The order for two 4-4-0 engines for the Cyprus Government Railway delivered in 1904 was the only export contract during that decade resulting in a loss which was minimal at half a per cent.

While the early 1900s were a time of good profit making there were concerns about the low prices and speedy delivery dates being promised by German and American manufacturers. The Secretary of State for India had received tenders from German firms which were twenty per cent below the British in price with delivery times of up to twenty-five weeks earlier.[36] Greg shared the view of other British manufacturers that British locomotives were superior in materials, workmanship and finish and also claimed that they were more fuel efficient and required fewer repairs. Hence the overall difference in cost was far less than at first seemed to be the case.[37] Government officials acknowledged those arguments yet remained impressed by the difference in price and delivery dates claiming that unless the latter were 'fully compensated for by the superior quality and durability' of the engines, the hitherto monopoly position of British manufacturers would be 'seriously imperilled'.[38] Foreign competition was to become increasingly intense especially during the inter-war period.

In the years leading up to the First World War and during the first year of conflict, export demand remained buoyant. Although only sixteen engines left the works in 1910, the export total for the six year period 1910 to 1915 amounted to 185, producing an average almost exactly the same as for the previous period. India accounted for nearly seventy per cent of exports and another twenty-two per cent were sent to Africa – Egypt, Uganda, South Africa, Sierra Leone and Nigeria. The three major customers were the Eastern Bengal Railway, the Jodhpur Bikaner Railway and Burma Railways. The profitability of contracts was less assured, however, with modest profit margins and occasional losses.

NW 908 (petrol engine) of 1910 for Morvi State Railway. (SLHL)

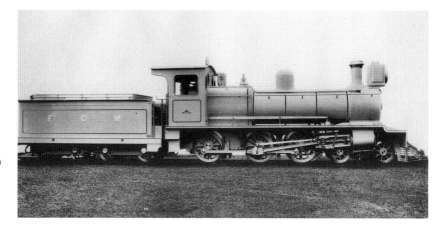

NW 911 of 1910 for Buenos Ayres Midland Railway. (SLHL)

NW 912 of 1910 for Earl of Ellesmere's Colliery. (SLHL)

NW 958 of 1912 for the County Donegal Railway at Derry, 1952. (D. Trevor Rowe)

In July 1915 the Bridgewater Foundry was declared a 'controlled establishment'. New locomotive contracts now required the permission of the Ministry of Munitions and munitions work was deemed a priority. A major Government order was made for the supply of 100 petrol-electric tractors of 2ft 8in gauge for use on the military railways in France. Each engine would weigh 7 tons 10cwt empty and have a fuel capacity of forty gallons of petrol. Many of the parts for these machines were bought in, such as the Clayton Shuttleworth radiators, the British Westinghouse generator motors and control gear and either 45bhp Tylor petrol engines or 38bhp Dorman petrol engines. The contract was worth £38,850 to the company. The War Office also ordered thirty-two 2-8-0 engines for the Railway Operating Division of the British Army for service in France. These locomotives were priced between £7,625 and £10,175 18s 1d. But, while the war brought new business to Patricroft, it also produced new problems as outlined in a letter from Greg to Lord Inverforth, Minister of Munitions in 1921. The letter concerned a contract, dated September 1915, to supply the French State Railways with twenty locomotives and tenders of the 'Standard French railways "Consolidation" type'. The order arose from the fact that most of the leading French locomotive works were either in enemy hands or destroyed, or devoting their energies to munitions production. The French contract was priced at £106,400 yet the firm ultimately suffered a loss of £12,235. This resulted from a variety of factors including the loss of workmen through enlistment, the inability to obtain materials such as tyres and steel castings and the sharp advance of wages that took place during the contract work.[39]

At the time that Nasmyth Wilson reconverted into a public company in August 1919 it was still a thriving locomotive business with useful subsidiary product lines. The premises had been completely updated during the previous fifteen years and the company enjoyed sound management both in the board room and on the shop floor. The only unsettling sign seemed to be the overwhelming dependence of the main product line on the export market. So anxious was the company to protect its export trade that when during the January 1910 general election campaign a local Conservative and tariff reformer, G.F. Assinder, had argued that free trade had led to a reduction in employment, Nasmyth's issued a manifesto to refute the claim. The company maintained that tariff reform would increase the cost of bought-in parts, such as boiler plates, copper plates and tubes, and would deal 'a serious, lasting, and probably irreparable blow to the business'[40] But just as worrying as the export dependence was the size of the business.

NW 1000 of 1913 for Bombay Port Trust, shown with company directors and employees. (SLHL)

Above: *NW 1008 of 1913 for Nigerian Railways. (SLHL)*

Opposite above: *NW 1089 of 1915 for Bengal Nagpur Railway at Motibagh, 1969. (Bawcutt Collection, National Railway Museum)*

Opposite below: *NW 1122 of 1916 for French State Railways. (SLHL)*

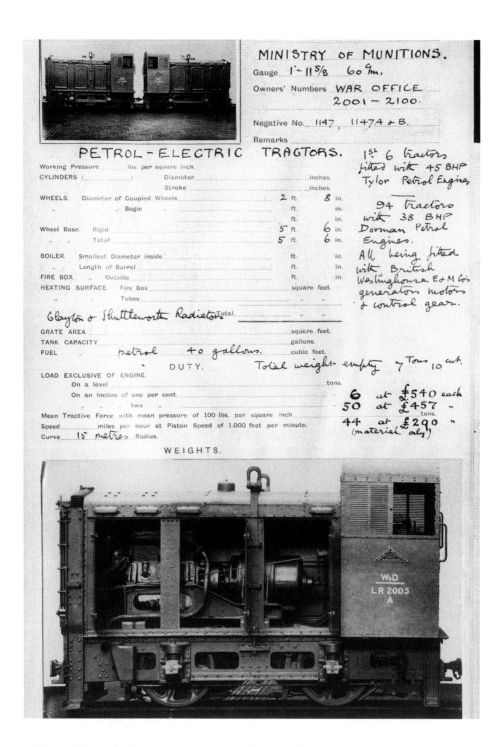

MINISTRY OF MUNITIONS.

Gauge 1'- 11⅝ 60 ᵍ/m.

Owners' Numbers WAR OFFICE
2001 – 2100.

Negative No. 1147, 1147A & B.

Remarks

PETROL - ELECTRIC TRACTORS.

1st 6 tractors fitted with 45 BHP Tylor Petrol Engines

94 tractors with 38 BHP Dorman Petrol Engines.

All being fitted with British Westinghouse E&M Co's generators motors & control gear.

Working Pressure	lbs. per square inch.			
CYLINDERS ( )	Diameter		inches.	
	Stroke		inches.	
WHEELS. Diameter of Coupled Wheels		2 ft.	8 in.	
" " Bogie		ft.	in.	
		ft.	in.	
Wheel Base. Rigid		5 ft.	6 in.	
" " Total		5 ft.	6 in.	
BOILER. Smallest Diameter inside		ft.	in.	
" Length of Barrel		ft.	in.	
FIRE BOX " Outside		ft.	in.	
HEATING SURFACE. Fire Box		square feet.		
" " Tubes		" "		
Clayton & Shuttleworth Radiator Total		" "		
GRATE AREA		square feet.		
TANK CAPACITY		gallons.		
FUEL " petrol 40 gallons.		cubic feet.		

DUTY.

Total weight empty 7 Tons 10 cwt.

LOAD EXCLUSIVE OF ENGINE.

On a level		tons.
On an incline of one per cent.		6 at £540 each
" two		50 at £457 "
Mean Tractive Force with mean pressure of 100 lbs. per square inch		tons.
Speed miles per hour at Piston Speed of 1,000 feet per minute.		44 at £290 "
Curve 15 metres Radius.		(material only)

WEIGHTS.

NW 1144-1243 of 1917 for Ministry of Munitions, specification book entry. (SLHL)

NW 1273 of 1919 for the Taff Vale Railway shown at Swindon, 1958. (D. Trevor Rowe)

While Nasmyth's was one of the leading locomotive builders it was also one of the smallest. In 1907, the year of maximum output by the private builders, the Bridgewater Foundry accounted for only four per cent of the total. The two local firms, Beyer Peacock and The Vulcan Foundry produced fourteen per cent and nine per cent respectively while the North British Locomotive Co. of Glasgow produced more than half the total output.[41] The industry had been steadily contracting in terms of the number of major builders since the 1840s. If further contraction should occur then Nasmyth's were now in the front line.

eight
Inter-war and Decline

In August 1919 Nasmyth's reconverted into a public company in order to increase the capital resources of the business. Why this was necessary remains unclear for the major expansion programme of 1903 to 1911 had been financed through bank loans and the issue of debenture stock so preserving the family-style nature of the firm. Perhaps the directors envisaged further modernization and expansion expecting the post-war boom conditions to continue. There were few signs until the second half of 1920 of a break in national prosperity. Whatever the reason, the existing £100 shares were subdivided into 100 £1 shares and the nominal capital increased to £200,000 by the creation of 100,000 new 8 per cent preference £1 shares. In December 1920 the capital was further increased to £300,000 by the creation of 100,000 £1 shares.[1] The issued capital stood at £23,600 eight per cent preference shares and £170,700 ordinary shares and this remained constant until 1940.

A controlling interest was obtained in Nasmyth's by the Sheffield steel manufacturing firm, John Brown & Co.[2] This was part of a long-established policy on behalf of Brown's to secure a number of captive markets – they had previously invested in Sharp Stewart & Co., Harland & Wolff and Cravens Railway Carriage & Wagon Company.[3] The Nasmyth investment would have provided an automatic outlet for the company's tyres, axles and springs. During the inter-war period two and sometimes three directors on Nasmyth's board were also directors of John Brown or Firth Brown as it became after the 1930 amalgamation. In 1922, in a boardroom of six, there were Allan John Grant (1875-1955) and Sir William Henry Ellis (1860-1945), while in 1937 there were Charles Spencer (c.1876-1940), Sir Holberry Mensforth (1871-1951) and Stanley Rawson (1891-1973).[4] Apart from Greg, the directors with a more immediate interest in the management of the factory were Reginald Wright, Vernon Gamon (1884-1937) and Robert Arbuthnott (1900-1980).

Wright had been a director since at least 1912 and his main function was that of overseas representative. When, in the autumn of 1920, Wright flew out to Romania in a D.H.9 Siddeley Puma of 230 h.p. on a month's mission, the local newspaper claimed that this was 'the first time an aeroplane has been used for a purely commercial purpose on so extended a journey'.[5] Gamon was a practical engineer becoming a pupil at Nasmyth's in 1901.[6] Between 1904 and 1908 he worked first for the Lancashire Dynamo & Motor Co., latterly as assistant works manager, and then Edison & Swan. He rejoined Nasmyth's in January 1909 as personal assistant to the active directors before joining the board in 1919. Arbuthnott was also an engineer by training, having served his apprenticeship at The Vulcan Foundry Ltd and later worked for the engineering section of the Glasgow Corporation Gas Department.[7] He came to Patricroft in 1926 as assistant works manager to James Bolas and took over as works manager in 1934. When Gamon died in November 1937, Arbuthnott became a director. Both these men held appointments suggesting they were highly regarded within their profession – Gamon was appointed director of the Manchester & District Engineering Employers Association in March 1937 and had been appointed to the Council of the Institution of Locomotive Engineers in 1933, while Arbuthnott became president of the Institution of Locomotive Engineers in 1958-1959 after relinquishing his position as joint managing director of North British Locomotive Co., the largest locomotive manufacturing company in Britain.

Above: *From left to right: Edward Hyde Greg (Managing Director), Reginald Wright (Sales Director) and James Bolas (Works Manager). (SLHL)*

Left: *Sir William Ellis (Director). (Institution of Civil Engineers)*

Above left: *Allan John Grant, Director. (Grant, 1950).*
Above right: *Vernon Gamon, Director, (Keith Gamon).*

Below left: *Robert Arbuthnott, Works Manager and Director, (Hugh J. Arbuthnott).*
Below right: *Donald Manson, Chief Draughtsman, (Ian Manson).*

NW 1268 of 1921 for Nasmyth Wilson & Co. Ltd. (SLHL)

During the inter-war years the product range at the Bridgewater Foundry remained unchanged, despite the growing threat to steam locomotive manufacturing activities posed by the expansion of road transport and the spread of railway electrification and diesel-driven locomotives. In their evidence to the Balfour Committee on Industry and Trade in 1925, the representatives of the LMA described the condition of the locomotive manufacturing industry as 'desperate'.[8] Yet while Nasmyth's experienced strong fluctuations in demand, their market performance for the decade as a whole was marginally above the average achieved for the period 1882 to 1919. Average annual production for the 1920s was 28.9 ranging between fifty-two locomotives in 1921, the highest annual total in the history of the business, and nineteen in 1923. In most years exports predominated with no domestic production taking place in seven out of the ten years. But exports slumped to eight engines in 1925 with the firm depending on domestic orders for the bulk of its locomotive custom in that year.

There were just four domestic customers during the 1920s. The Astley & Tyldesley Colliery received an 0-8-0 tank engine named *Emanuel Clegg* and the Bridgewater Foundry itself received a crane locomotive for internal use named *James Nasmyth*. The latter was the only crane locomotive built by the company and was invoiced at £4,605. It was designed to lift five tons around a radius of 14ft and could achieve a speed of 31.2mph. The main domestic business came from the Great Northern Railway of Ireland and the recently formed London, Midland & Scottish Railway. Both companies ordered fifteen locomotives and an 0-4-4 tank engine delivered to the Tilbury section of the last named company would have been the last delivery made to a domestic customer. Henceforth, all the locomotives that left the works were for the export market.

As with the period leading up to the First World War, India and Burma constituted the principal export market between 1920 and 1929 accounting for nearly eighty per cent of

NW 1303 of 1920 for South Indian Railway at Lalgudi, 1969. (Bawcutt Collection, National Railway Museum)

export sales. Africa, particularly West Africa, accounted for nearly seventeen per cent. In total, 257 locomotives were exported during these years with the most important customers being the South Indian Railway (forty-three engines), the Burma Railway (twenty-nine engines) and Nigerian Railways (twenty-three engines). Of the twenty-nine customers, nine received ten or more machines. Perhaps the most remarkable engines constructed during this period on account of their size and weight were the two 5ft 6in gauge, 106 ton, 2-10-2 tank engines for the Bombay Port Trust delivered in 1921. The two engines together were priced at £26,734 13s 7d and the contract made a profit of ten per cent. The profit/loss data for this period covers ninety-four exported locomotives and unfortunately comes to an end in 1922. The data demonstrates, however, the excellent profits to be gained from export orders placed in the immediate post-war era. Every contract made a profit and for sixty-four of the ninety-four locomotives documented, the profit margins exceeded thirty per cent with the most profitable contract being the thirty-eight per cent profit earned on two 4-6-0 engines, priced £9,936 each, supplied to the South Indian Railway in 1922. The average profit margin on the ninety-four locomotives was over twenty-seven per cent. It seems highly probable that these favourable terms of trade deteriorated towards the mid-1920s. In 1925 only five engines were exported. But there were few signs in the late 1920s that disaster was just around the corner and eighty-five engines were dispatched in the three-year period 1927 to 1929.

There is very little evidence relating to non-locomotive work undertaken by the company during the 1920s. Cotton presses and boilers continued to be staple products, as did steam hammers, but the output of the latter fell to a total of thirteen compared to seventy-one during the previous decade. Because of the stability of the product range there was little scope for innovation except in improving existing processes and designs. In 1921 and 1930 the company

NW 1357 of 1922 for Bombay Port Trust. (SLHL)

NW 1358 of 1922 for Bombay Port Trust at Wadala, Bombay, 1974. (L.G. Marshall)

NW 1368 of 1921 for Bombay Port Trust at Wadala, Bombay, 1974. (L.G. Marshall)

NW 1374 of 1922 for Bengal Nagpur Railway at Ranchi, 1975. (L.G. Marshall)

obtained patents, taken out in conjunction with their chief draughtsman, Donald Manson (1866-1935)[9], for improving the construction of blower valves for creating the draught in the flues of steam locomotive boilers (this involved recycling used steam – a form of fuel economy), and improvements in the construction of double-bogie locomotives such that they did not roll off the track at bends on account of their unusual length. These were the last patents obtained by the company.

In October 1929 the economic prosperity of the late 1920s finally came to an end with the Wall Street Crash which marked the onset of prolonged depression. In 1930, the value of British locomotive exports was £3.75 million, representing 50,565 tons, and this dropped to £370,000 in 1932, representing 3,873 tons.[10] Although there was then some recovery, the value of exports in 1937, £1.1 million, was still only thirty per cent of the 1930 figure.[11] The export problems of the British locomotive building industry were exacerbated by a number of factors, including the development of locomotive building capacities by Australia and New Zealand and the advance in German competition. It was widely suspected that German firms were in receipt of government subsidies since tendering prices were sometimes below the British costs of production.[12] Currency fluctuations, the Sino-Japanese war and poor harvests in the Argentine all added to the export difficulties of British firms. Even when orders were secured, the profit margins were often minimal on account of the fierce competition and the increase in steel costs due to rearmament. The chairman of Armstrong-Whitworth informed a general meeting of his company in May 1937 of 'the virtual impossibility of getting remunerative prices for export orders'.[13] At home the reduction in demand was compounded by schemes for the more intensive working of steam locomotives involving improvements to track and turntables, arrangements

NW 1375 of 1922 for Bengal Nagpur Railway at Gangiwara, 1969. (Bawcutt Collection, National Railway Museum)

NW1407 of 1923 for South Indian Railway at Trichy, 1969.
(Bawcutt Collection, National Railway Museum)

for the speeding up of the replenishment of coal and water supplies, and improved signalling.[14] There was also a steady fall in the number of steam locomotives in use partly due to the increase in the number of electric rail-motor vehicles.[15]

The combined impact of all these factors on the Bridgewater Foundry was to reduce orders and convert a thriving business into a loss-making concern. In 1921, following the post-war boom in business, the balance on the profit and loss account was £54,683.[16] By 1929 this had dropped to £13,145. During the period 1930 to 1933 losses of £14,232, £11,255 and £17,593 were sustained.[17] In terms of locomotive business, a total of seventy-six engines were built between 1930 and 1938. The peak year was 1936 when seventeen locomotives were produced, while in 1931 and 1933 only two engines left the factory. As in the previous period, India constituted the principal market accounting for forty-two per cent of deliveries followed by Africa with twenty-two per cent. New custom was found in China (twelve engines)[18] and Palestine (eleven engines) and four locomotives were sent to Jamaica. Only two customers received more than ten engines, the Bengal & North Western Railway and Palestine Railways.

With the private locomotive-building firms barred from access to the home market by the railway company workshops and with what appeared to be a permanent reduction in export demand, there was a problem of over-capacity in the British locomotive building industry during the 1930s. At a special meeting of the LMA, attended by both Greg and Gamon, in January 1937, Alec Campbell of the Hunslet Engine Co. stated that 'unless the Industry were reorganized so that those remaining in the Industry could be placed on an economic footing, the private locomotive building industry in Great Britain would go to the wall'. Nasmyth's were a prime candidate for elimination in a rationalization of the industry for the company was described at a general meeting of the LMA in December 1937 as 'competitively on the fringe' of the market. The scale of locomotive building at the Bridgewater Foundry was insufficient to justify the continuation of its locomotive business given the interests of the industry as a whole. Accordingly, a purchase of Nasmyth Wilson's locomotive business was negotiated between the Locomotive Manufacturers Co. Ltd and the Nasmyth board for £70,000 on 23 December 1937. Nasmyth's could continue as general engineers but were now obliged to cease locomotive production and hand over all 'drawings, patterns, blocks & co.' relating to the building and repair of locomotives and boilers. The buy-out was funded by a three per cent contract levy imposed on the remaining members of the LMA.[19]

While the company continued to trade in steam hammers and other engineering equipment, the heart had now gone out of the business which continued to make a loss – £2,663 for the year ending 31 December 1939.[20] It was perhaps fortunate both for the shareholders and the workforce that the onset of war enabled the business to become absorbed by the Ministry of Supply. On 1 June 1940, the Bridgewater Foundry became the Royal Ordnance Factory, Patricroft, and by a special resolution passed on 7 November 1940 the concern went into voluntary liquidation. Henceforth, the factory premises would be devoted to the production of guns, tanks and other sinews of war. In April 1987 the ROF was bought from the Government by British Aerospace and, in 1989, as part of another rationalisation programme, the factory closed for the last time. It is now part of a business and technology centre.[21]

There can be little doubt that Nasmyth Wilson was an extremely successful locomotive building concern retaining a profitable business until the late 1920s. Only a handful of

NW 1436 of 1924 for the Great Northern Railway of Ireland at Portadown, 1955.
(L. G. Marshall)

competitors could match this record and Nasmyth Wilson's very longevity suggests that it must have been one of the most progressive engineering firms of the period, a view supported by regular reports in the technical press. The companies that survived the depression such as North British and Beyer Peacock continued for another twenty years but all the main contractors had ceased trading by the early 1960s. The secrets of Nasmyth Wilson's success lay partly in the decisions of its founders with regard to location, capitalisation, construction of appropriate premises and the achievement of a broad product range. Unfortunately, the impetus of invention and innovation was not sustained after the death of Robert Wilson in 1882, though the firm was still able to prosper by concentrating on locomotive manufacture with emphasis upon improving production and marketing techniques. With the benefit of hindsight it is possible to see that the Bridgewater Foundry was becoming dangerously dependent not just on one line of business but on the export markets. The immediate post-war years would have been the time for product variation and the cultivation of home-market custom. Yet this would almost certainly have detracted from what at the time appeared to be an extremely profitable trade in steam locomotives. Ultimately, Nasmyth Wilson became a victim of its own success.

NW 1459 of 1925 for the London Midland & Scottish Railway at Polmadie Shed, 1961. (L.W. Rowe)

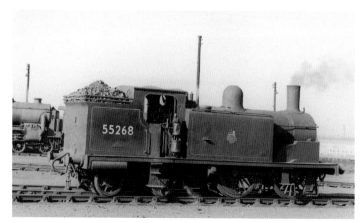

NW 1461 of 1925 for the London Midland & Scottish Railway. (L.G. Marshall Collection)

NW 1472 of 1926 for Nigerian Railways. (SLHL)

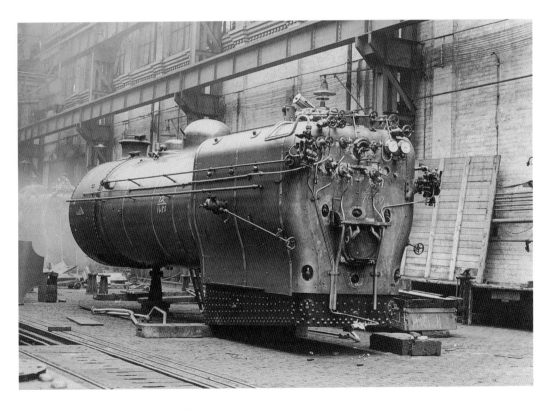

Spare boiler for India. (SLHL)

*NW 1485 of 1926
for Barsi Light Railway
at Kurduwadi, 1975.
(L.G. Marshall)*

*NW 1494 of 1927
for Nigerian Railways.
(SLHL)*

*NW 1516 of
1927 for Eastern
Bengal Railway at
Kathgodam, 1979.
(L.G.Marshall)*

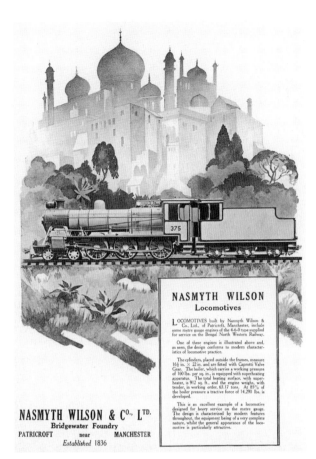

NASMYTH WILSON
Locomotives

LOCOMOTIVES built by Nasmyth Wilson & Co., Ltd., of Patricroft, Manchester, include some metre gauge engines of the 4-6-0 type supplied for service on the Bengal North Western Railway.

One of these engines is illustrated above and, as seen, the design conforms to modern characteristics of locomotive practice.

The cylinders, placed outside the frames, measure 16½ in. × 22 in. and are fitted with Caprotti Valve Gear. The boiler, which carries a working pressure of 160 lbs. per sq. in., is equipped with superheating apparatus. The total heating surface, with superheater, is 912 sq. ft., and the engine weighs, with tender, in working order, 63.17 tons. At 85% of the boiler pressure a tractive force of 14,290 lbs. is developed.

This is an excellent example of a locomotive designed for heavy service on the metre gauge. The design is characterised by modern features throughout, the equipment being of a very complete nature, whilst the general appearance of the locomotive is particularly attractive.

NASMYTH WILSON & C⁰., L™.
Bridgewater Foundry
PATRICROFT   near   MANCHESTER
Established 1836

Left: *Advertisement featuring NW 1530 of 1928 for Bengal North Western Railway.* (The Railway Gazette, *1928*)

Below: *NW 1531 of 1928 for India North Western Railway. (SLHL)*

NW 1537/8 of 1928 for Bengal Dooars Railway. (SLHL)

NW 1543 of 1928 for Barsi Light Railway at Shendri, 1980. (L.G. Marshall)

NW 1564 of 1929 for Bengal Nagpur Raipur Dhamtari Railway. (SLHL)

*NW 1564 of 1929 for Bengal Nagpur Raipur Dhamtari Railway at Abhanpur Junction, 1975.
(L.G. Marshall)*

NW 1576 of 1929 for Barsi Light Railway. (SLHL)

NW 1579 of 1930 for Mysore State Railway at Shimoga Town Depot, 1973. (L.G. Marshall)

Probably one of NW 1580-1585 of 1930 for Kenya & Uganda Railway crossing Barton swing bridge. (SLHL)

Probably one of NW 1580-1585 of 1930 for Kenya & Uganda Railway en route to Manchester Docks. The sign on the back of the trailer reads, 'You are behind the world's largest lorry. Please drive with caution'. (SLHL)

One of series NW 1588-1591 of 1930 for Tanganyika Railway leaving the Bridgewater Foundry. (SLHL)

NW 1588-1591 of 1930 for Tanganyika Railway awaiting shipment. (SLHL)

Opposite above*: One of series NW 1588-1591 being lifted aboard ship. (SLHL)*

Opposite below: *NW 1594-1601 of 1932 for Tientsin Pukow Railway, general arrangement drawings. (The* Railway Engineer, *January 1933)*

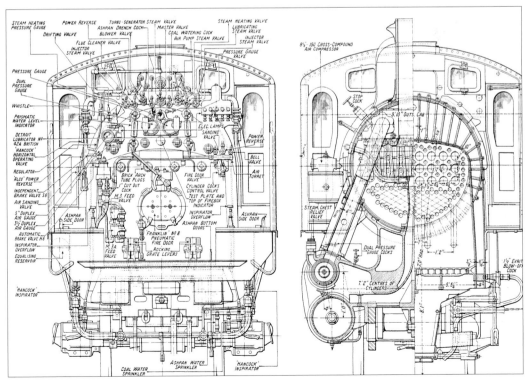

STEAM HEATING
PRESSURE GAUGE — POWER REVERSE — TURBO-GENERATOR STEAM VALVE — STEAM HEATING VALVE
DRIFTING VALVE — ASHPAN DRENCH COCK — MASTER VALVE — LUBRICATING STEAM VALVE
BLOWER VALVE — COAL WATERING COCK — INJECTOR STEAM VALVE
FLUE CLEANER VALVE — AIR PUMP STEAM VALVE — PRESSURE GAUGE VALVE
INJECTOR STEAM VALVE

8½ - 150 CROSS-COMPOUND AIR COMPRESSOR

PRESSURE GAUGE

DUAL PRESSURE GAUGE

WHISTLE

PRISMATIC WATER LEVEL INDICATOR

DETROIT LUBRICATOR Nº 42A BRITISH

'HANCOCK' HORIZONTAL OPERATING VALVE

REGULATOR

'ALCO' POWER REVERSE

INDEPENDENT BRAKE VALVE S.6

AIR SANDING VALVE

5" DUPLEX AIR GAUGE

3½" DUPLEX AIR GAUGE

AUTOMATIC BRAKE VALVE H.6

INSPIRATOR OVERFLOW

EQUALISING RESERVOIR

'HANCOCK' INSPIRATOR

ELEC. LAMPS
SANDING VALVE

POWER REVERSE

BELL VALVE

AIR TURRET

BRICK ARCH TUBE PLUGS
1" CUT OUT COCK

FIRE DOOR VALVE

CYLINDER COCKS CONTROL VALVE

TEST PLATE AND TOP OF FIREBOX INDICATOR

INSPIRATOR OVERFLOW

ASHPAN SIDE DOOR

ASHPAN SIDE DOOR

M.3 FEED VALVE

FRANKLIN Nº 8 PNEUMATIC FIRE DOOR

ASHPAN BOTTOM DOORS

M.3A FEED VALVE

ROCKING GRATE LEVERS

STOP COCK

9'.10" OUTS. CAB

STEAM CHEST RELIEF VALVE

DUAL PRESSURE GAUGE COCKS

7'.2" CENTRES OF CYLINDERS

1½" EVRIT BLOW-OFF COCK

COAL WATER SPRINKLER

ASHPAN WATER SPRINKLER

'HANCOCK' INSPIRATOR

Left: *Front of one of series NW 1594-1601 of 1932 for Tientsin Pukow Railway. (SLHL)*

Below: *Footplate of one of series NW 1594-1601 of 1932 for Tientsin Pukow Railway. (SLHL)*

NW 1597 of 1932 for Tientsin Pukow Railway at Patricroft Station awaiting movement to Weaste Siding junction with the Manchester Ship Canal lines. (SLHL)

NW 1594 of 1932 for Tientsin Pukow Railway being lifted aboard ship. (SLHL)

Opposite above: *NW 1598 of 1932 for Tientsin Pukow Railway being pulled by a London Midland & Scottish engine to Salford Docks. (SLHL)*

Opposite below: *NW 1609 of 1935 for Palestine Railways. (SLHL)*

NW 1627 of 1936 for Gold Coast Government Railways. (SLHL)

NW 1638 of 1936 for Bhavnagar State Railway at Bhavnagar Para Depot, 1973. (L.G. Marshall)

NW 1648 of 1937 for Bengal & North Western Railway at Lucknow Junction, 1979. (L.G. Marshall)

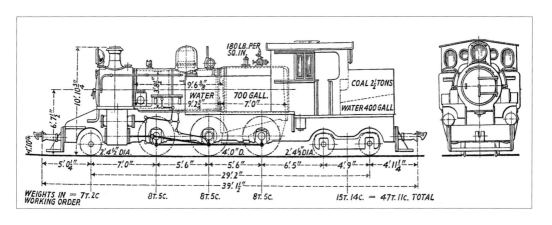

*General arrangement drawing of series NW 1649 and 1650 of 1938 for South Indian Railway. (*The Railway Gazette, *January 1939)*

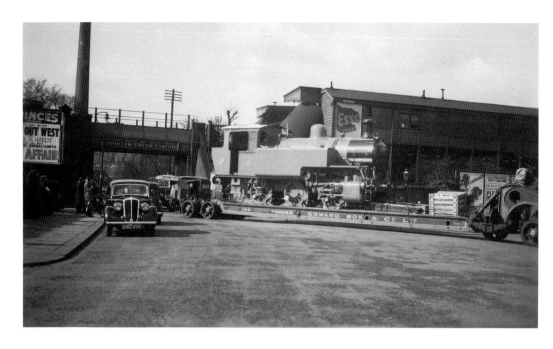

NW 1651 of 1938 for Palestine Railways passing Patricroft Station. (SLHL)

NW 1651 of 1938 for Palestine Railways in Manchester city centre. (SLHL)

Endnotes

Chapter one

1 For a detailed description of these locomotives see *The Railway Gazette*, 20 January 1939, pp.103-104.

2 The Hunslet Engine Co. of Leeds purchased the goodwill of Kerr Stuart & Co. of Stoke-on-Trent in 1930 and the goodwill, drawings, patterns and stock of the Avonside Engine Co. in 1935. In 1937 there was a major reorganisation amongst the Tyneside builders when R.&W. Hawthorn Leslie & Co. merged with R. Stephenson & Co. and Armstrong-Whitworth agreed to cease locomotive production. Kitson's of Leeds followed the path of Nasmyth's in 1938. For a summary of the restructuring of the locomotive industry in the 1930s see the *Financial Times*, 8 March 1938, *The Engineer*, vol.165, 18 March 1938, p.295 and PEP (1951), pp. 17-19.

3 The Vulcan Foundry had traded since 1833, R. Stephenson & Co. since 1825 and Hawthorn Leslie & Co. since 1831. Lowe (1975), p.9.

4 By the end of 1938 The Vulcan Foundry and Beyer Peacock had produced 4,775 and 6,860 locomotives respectively and the major builders had produced 49,247. Nasmyth's output represents 3.3 per cent of this total. Figures derived from Atkins (1999), pp.122-123.

5 *The Railway Gazette*, reprinted supplement (nd), pp.3 & 10.

6 *The Railway Gazette*, 20 January 1939, p.89.

7 Smiles (1863). There is brief mention in this work of other early locomotive manufacturers such as Matthew Murray, Richard Roberts and William Fairbairn.

8 Smiles (1883).

9 *The Ironmonger* (1887), p.61. Prior to the 1880s, locomotive sales were occasionally the main component of turnover, as in 1841 and 1842, but this was not a sustainable position; there were no locomotive sales, for example, in 1843 and 1844.

10 For a history of Nasmyth's during James Nasmyth's years at the helm, 1836 to 1856, see Cantrell (1984). Moore (1981) has produced an illustrated list of the locomotives manufactured at the Bridgewater Foundry 1838-1938. For a brief, but not always accurate, summary of the firm's early locomotive activities see C.E. Clement, 'James Nasmyth's Early Locomotives', *The Mechanical World*, 2 March 1900. More reliable is *The Railway Gazette* (1913) pp.779-790 and 'Short histories of famous firms. No. III: Nasmyth, Wilson & Co., Ltd.,' *The Engineer*, vol.29, 19 March 1920, pp.287-289. For the other major builders see K. Warren (1989) – *Armstrong Whitworth & Co.*, Baker & Civil (1973) – *W.G. Bagnall Ltd*, R. Wear (1990) – *Andrew Barclay Sons & Co.*, Hume & Moss (1979) – *W. Beardmore & Co.*, Hills & Patrick (1982) – *Beyer Peacock & Co.*, Clarke (1978) – *Hawthorn Leslie & Co.*, Redman (1972) – *Hudswell Clarke Ltd*, Rolt (1964) and Townsley (1998) – *Hunslet Engine Co.*, Kitson Clark (1938) – *Kitson & Co.*, Bradley (1995), Campbell (1978) and Fleming, McKinstry & Wallace (2000) – *North British Locomotive Co.*, J.G.H. Warren (1923) – *Robert Stephenson & Co.* and The Locomotive Publishing Co. (1930) – *The Vulcan Foundry Co.* As yet there are no histories of the firms that merged to form North British in 1903: Neilson & Co., Dübs & Co. and Sharp Stewart & Co. For the early years of the latter firm see Hills (2002). There are short histories of all the steam locomotive manufacturers in Lowe (1975).

11 Nasmyth locomotives can still be found in many of their market destinations including England (Midland Railway Centre, Butterley, Derbyshire), Ireland (Foyle Valley Museum, Derry and the Ulster Folk & Transport Museum, Belfast), India (National Rail Museum, New Delhi), Kenya (Jamhuri Park, Nairobi) and New Zealand (Hooterville Heritage Trust, Waitara, Ohai Railway Board Heritage Trust,

Southland, etc.). The Midland Railway Centre Nasmyth locomotive (Works No. 454) was built in 1894 and delivered to Brown Bailey Co's steel works in Sheffield. It has not been restored to working order but becomes a star attraction during the museum's 'Friends of Thomas the Tank Engine' events when the 0-4-0 saddle tank takes on the identity of *Oswald the Talking Engine* for the amusement of future generations of railway enthusiasts.

12 Most of the business records relating to Nasmyth Wilson are held by Salford Archives. The most important items comprise a locomotive specification book c.1867-1922 with photographs of locomotive types between nos. 120-1382, order books 1836-1859, sales books 1837-1861 and 1870-1877, letter books 1838-1840 and 1875-1878 and two memorandum books of W.M. Wilson c.1886-1894. There are two files at the PRO containing occasional summaries of capital and shares, particulars of directors, annual returns and various legal documents relating to the structure of the firm. The National Railway Museum holds two specification books for the period 1867-1938 (with accompanying photographs) together with a collection (92 items) of coloured general arrangement drawings of locomotives and tenders for the period 1917-1938.

Chapter two

1 George Nasmyth was written out of the record by his younger brother on account of a professional disgrace. For a reconstruction of his life see Cantrell (2003).

2 For short introductions to James Nasmyth see Musson & Robinson (1969), pp.489-509 and Cantrell & Cookson eds. (2002), pp.129-146. For a longer study see Cantrell (1984).

3 Cooksey (1991)

4 Unless otherwise stated the information on James Nasmyth's early life is drawn from Smiles (1883).

5 Proposal dated 19 March 1828, National Library of Scotland, Dep.230, Box 68.

6 In fact, Nasmyth mistook the *Rocket* for the *Northumbrian*. Even allowing for the possibly distorted perspective from the top of Edge Hill cutting which might account for the repositioning of the cylinders (from upright to horizontal), the firebox and other details reveal Nasmyth's error. I am grateful to Michael Bailey for advice on this point.

7 James Nasmyth to David Octavius Hill, 5 August 1835, Royal Observatory Edinburgh.

8 Schedule of deeds relating to property held at Patricroft by Nasmyth and to partnership agreements between 31 Dec. 1835 and 1 Oct. 1867, SLHL, SN23,55.

9 There is no full length study of Holbrook Gaskell. For shorter assessments see Cantrell (1981), pp.353-355, Cantrell (1984), pp. 36-60, Dickenson (1956), pp.95-104, *The Engineer*, vol. 107 (1909), p.266 and entries in the *DNB* and *Dictionary of Business Biography*. Unless otherwise stated the information for the remainder of this chapter is drawn from Cantrell (1981), pp.346-358.

10 Hunter Gaskell to H. Gaskell, undated but probably 1844, SA, U313/C2/1-2.

11 James Nasmyth to Charles Babbage, 2 November 1850, BL, Add.37194, f.432.

12 Clark (1978).

13 It later became known as the 'Tower Building'. It was demolished in 1974 as it had become unsafe and a fire hazard. *EPJ*, 18 September 1974.

14 See pp. 74

15 Henry Garnett to James Nasmyth, 8 January 1877, BL, Add.71075, f.96.

Chapter three

1 Smiles (1883), pp.202-206.

2 J. Nasmyth to H. Gaskell, 11 July 1836, SA, U313/C4/1.

3 Love &Barton (1839), pp.213-219.

4 Ordnance Survey 1848 (surveyed 1845), six inches to the mile, Lancashire Sheet 103.

5 Cantrell (1984), p.33.

6 Love & Barton (1839), p.214.

7 *Engineering*, vol.3, 8 February 1867, p.124.

8 *The Engineer*, vol.25, 1867, p.360.

9 *PIME*, July 1894, p.436-8.

10 *The Ironmonger* (1887), p.60.

11 The following description of the new machine shop is drawn from an account in *Engineering*, vol.3, 22 March 1867, p.265.

12 See note 9.

13 See note 10.

14 The following description of the Bridgewater Foundry is based on the account in *The Railway Gazette* (1913), pp. 779-790 and the reprinted supplement (nd), pp. 3-10.

15 An enlarged portrait of James Nasmyth flanked by many pictures of locomotive engines was displayed in the board room. *EPJ*, 10 May 1907.

16 A local newspaper correspondent observed that over a hundred different drawings had to be made for every locomotive design involving up to two months of work. *EPJ*, 10 May 1907.

17 See note 7.

18 See note 9.

19 See p.130 note 21.

Chapter four

1 Cantrell (1984), p.229.

2 Atkins (1999), p.57.

3 *PIME*, June 1929, p.729.

4 Smiles (1883), pp.214-216.

5 Cantrell (1984), p.54.

6 *Ibid*, pp.231-232.

7 *Ibid*, p.232.

8 *EPJ*, 16 September 1898 and 6 September 1907.

9 *Ibid*, 24 December 1884.

10 *Ibid*, 19 December 1902.

11 Smiles (1883), pp. 206 and 216.

12 Board of Health Report, Barton-upon-Irwell.

13 Lord Seymour to James Nasmyth, 27 July 1854, Edinburgh City Library.

14 Cantrell (1984), p. 230.

15 *EPJ*, 25 February 1938.

16 *Ibid*, 26 October 1978. Albert Edward Platts (1893-1985) became foreman of the erecting shop in 1929 having been laid off during the 1920s. He retained this position until 1940 when he transferred to The Vulcan Foundry.

17 Cantrell (1984), p.237.

18 James Nasmyth to Rachel Chadwick, 2 May 1852, Chadwick MSS, University College, London.

19 Cantrell (1984), p.239. The youngest employee of Nasmyth living in one of the foundry cottages at the time of the 1851 census was Wright Lee, aged nine, an iron dresser. The average age of the 110 workers inhabiting these cottages in 1851 was 31.

20 Cantrell (1984), pp.240-243.

21 *EPJ*, 7 February 1874.

22 *Ibid*, 11 November 1892.

23 Burgess (1975), pp.60-71.

24 *EPJ*, 27 January 1912.

25 Weinbren (1995), pp.31-32.

26 *Ibid*, p.33.

Chapter five

1 Nasmyth claimed that between 1842 and 1852 the railway company workshops had absorbed between 10,000 and 12,000 skilled mechanics from the general labour market forcing wage rates up by fifteen per cent. J. Nasmyth to Edwin Chadwick, 2 May 1852, Chadwick MSS, University College, London.

2 Atkins (1999), p.22.

3 Smiles (1883), p.286.

4 Cantrell (1984), pp.166-167.

5 The Hilton's paper-making mills were amongst the largest in the world.

6 This took place shortly after the outbreak of the Second World War when the business archive of the Bridgewater Foundry was carted off for pulping as part of the Waste Paper Drive. The partial survival of the records was due to the timely action of Robert Arbuthnott (see p.98) who managed to rescue some of the most important items.

7 NG & Co. to John Moss, chairman of Grand Junction Railway, 5 March 1839, LB4, 206, SA, U268/C1/3.

8 J. Nasmyth to H. Gaskell, 12 July 1836, SA, U313/C4/2.

9 These were Works Nos. 1, 8, 9 & 10.

10 NG & Co. to Robert Garnett, 10 September 1838, LB5, 393, SA, U268/C1/4.

11 No.1, the *Bridgewater* fetched £950, No.8, *Wolf*, £1,261, and the two engines *Nasmyth* and *Patricroft* (Nos. 9 & 10) sold to Darwen Mills, approximately £1,030 each. The three last named locomotives had been offered to the Birmingham & Gloucester Railway for £1,500 each in March 1839.

12 The distinguishing features of the Bury locomotives were bar frames of forged iron, four wheels, either 2-2-0 or 0-4-0, with the 'D' pattern, domed-top firebox behind the rear axle.

13 Smiles (1883), p.182.

14 NG & Co. to E. Bury, 27 July 1838, LB2, 348, SA, U268/C1/1.

15 NG & Co. to T. Cooke, 7 August 1838, LB2, 383, SA, U268/C1/1.

16 NG & Co. to E. Bury, 31 October 1838, LB3, 196, SA, U268/C1/2.

17 NG & Co. to E. Bury, 17 December 1838 and 10 January 1839, LB3, 367 and 439, SA, U268/C1/2.

18 NG & Co. to E. Bury, 19 July 1839, LB5, 238, SA, U268/C1/4.

19 NG & Co. to E. Bury, 31 July 1839, LB5, 282, SA, U268/C1/4.

20 NG & Co. to E. Bury, 19 February 1840, LB7, 187, SA, U268/C1/6.

21 NG & Co. to E. Bury, 5 June 1839, LB5, 43, SA, U268/C1/4.

22 *The Locomotive Magazine*, 14 February 1903.

23 NG & Co. to S.J. Woods, 11 and 16 February 1839, LB4, 143 and 158, SA, U268/C1/3.

24 Order Book 1, p.48, SA, U268/F1/1.

25 NG & Co. to S.J. Woods, 27 February 1839, LB4, 183, SA, U268/C1/3.

26 NG & Co. to S.J. Woods, 19 September 1839, LB5, 433, SA, U268/C1/4.

27 NG & Co. to S.J. Woods, 20 January 1840, LB7, 35, SA, U268/C1/6.

28 NG & Co. to S.J. Woods, 11 November 1839, LB6, 189, SA, U268/C1/5.

29 NG & Co. to T.L. Gooch, 8 December 1838, LB3, 330, SA, U268/C1/2.

30 NG & Co. to J. Jellicose, 7 March 1839, LB4,212, SA, U268/C1/3.

31 NG & Co. to J. Todd, 13 September 1839, LB5, 414, SA, U269/C1/4.

32 Order Book 1, p.87, SA, U268/F1/1.

33 NG & Co. to the Birmingham & Gloucester Railway, 14 December 1840, quoted in Dewhurst (1947-1949).

34 Document dated 23 December 1840 quoted in Dewhurst (1947-1949).

35 Sales Book A, pp.137, 143, 152, 164, 166 & 175, SA, U269/F2/1.

36 *Ibid*, p.181.

37 The locomotives were of the Firefly class based on Robert Stephenson's design.

38 *The Locomotive Magazine*, August 1901.

39 *Ibid*, June 1901.

40 According to Stretton (1900), the company was so surprised at the firm's low bidding price for the contract that it decided there was some mistake and arranged a meeting with James Nasmyth. The £100 bonus was the result of this discussion.

41 J. Nasmyth to I.K. Brunel, 13 June 1843, Bodleian Library, Oxford.

42 I.K. Brunel to Messrs Maudslay & Field, 20 December 1841, Bristol University Library.

43 NG & Co., to the chairman of the Great Western Railway, 4 March 1841, BTC Archives HL 1/12.1E.

44 Dyos & Aldcroft (1969), pp.132-139.

45 Order Book 1, pp.205-206, SA, U268/F1/1.

46 Sales Book B, p.39, SA, U268/F2/2.

47 Order Book 1, p.288, SA, U268/F1/1.

48 Marshall (1978), p.210.

49 The first patent (No. 8023, 9 April 1839) was for encircling locomotive bearings or journals with collars or rings of case-hardened iron or hardened steel, instead of brasses. This improvement was adopted on the engines built for stock and manufacturers were charged a total of £100 to use the patent or £1 per locomotive. The second patent (No. 8299, 4 December 1839) was for an arrangement of self-acting brakes for railway carriages. See Cantrell (1984), pp.119-120.

50 All the figures on locomotive output are derived from the various statistical tables in Atkins (1999), pp.15, 22 & 122.

Chapter six

1 H. Garnett to J. Nasmyth, 8 January 1877, BL, Add.71075, f.96.

2 See pp. 24-26

3 Benjamin Wilson is described as first a mariner (1799) and then a cooper (1803) in the Dunbar Parish Register. Robert Wilson described his father's occupation as a cooper on his marriage certificate of 26 May 1845. It would be quite natural to combine these occupations, for barrels were in constant demand during the herring seasons.

4 Robert Wilson erected a memorial to his parents, sisters and two of his children in Dunbar Kirk Yard. Monument No. A315.

5 EPJ, 7 February 1874.

6 R. Wilson to H. Gaskell, 7 December 1864, SA, U313/C5/4.

7 According to Fleeming Jenkin's obituary notice (see Note 35) Wilson began working at this address in 1832. Gray's Edinburgh Directory records a Robert Wilson, machine maker, at 16 Paul's Work between 1835 and 1838.

8 Both the DNB and Fleeming Jenkin's obituary notice state that Wilson moved to Patricroft in 1838.

9 Robert Wilson's second daughter, Rachel Smith Wilson was baptised in Scotland in June 1839.

10 See Note 5. The first references to Wilson in the firm's order book and petty cash book are for November and October 1840 respectively.

11 Smiles (1863), pp.282-291.

12 Rowlandson (1864).

13 J. Nasmyth to S. Smiles, 31 July 1882, BL, Add. 71076, f.153.

14 J. Nasmyth to S. Smiles, 25 May 1881, BL, Add. 71076, ff.39-40.

15 Cantrell (1985).

16 There are no statistics for steam engines but 313 stationary boilers were produced between 1857 and 1882, see Note 22.

17 Engineering, vol.3 (1867), p.124.

18 British Patent No. 2,577, 3 November 1856.

19 British Patent No. 2,436, 6 July 1875.

20 Advertising Leaflet, SLHL, SN27.

21 British Patent No. 2,663, 28 June 1876.

22 There is a list of presses (1853-1890) and stationary boilers (1838-1887) manufactured at Patricroft in a miscellaneous notebook kept by W.M. Wilson (probably William Mclean Wilson, a son of Robert Wilson senior), SA, U268/B3/1.

23 The first reference to this company is dated 28 March 1872, Sales Book E, p.114, SA, U268/F2/4.

24 J.G.H. Warren, 'John Nuttall's Sketch Book', TNS., vol. 11 (1830-31), pp.67-89.

25 *PICE*, vol.126, 1896, pp.394-395.

26 For a full list of Robert Wilson's patents see Cantrell (1984), p.263.

27 Wilson's third wife, Mary Gibson (1825-1871) was the sister of John Lancaster's wife, Euphemia Gibson. John Lancaster (1815-1884) was the Chairman of the Wigan Coal & Iron Co., 1865-70, and MP for Wigan, 1868-1874.

28 The combined price of each locomotive and tender was £2085.

29 These were priced between £1,222 and £1,236 depending on whether the delivery point was Liverpool or London.

30 For a more detailed account of the rolling stock supplied to Majorca see Barnabe (2003), pp.43-51.

31 Atkins (1999), p.21.

32 *Ibid*, pp.122-123.

33 British Patent No. 3,652, 8 September 1880.

34 *Manchester City News*, 15 January 1898.

35 *Proceedings of the Royal Society of Edinburgh*, vol.14, 1886-1887.

Chapter seven

1 Nasmyth Wilson & Co. Ltd., Memorandum of Association, 25 April 1882, TNA, BT31/40370/16751/1.

2 For a brief financial history of the company, 1882-1927, see *Morning Post*, 28 November, 1927.

3 Nasmyth Wilson & Co. Ltd., Summary of Capital and Shares, 2 August 1882, TNA, BT31/40370/16751/6.

4 William Smethurst (1850-1940) was chief draughtsman at Nasmyth's between 1879 and 1896 following an education at Kirkham Grammar School and the Manchester Mechanics' Institution. He was apprenticed to Sharp, Stewart & Co. Ltd., Manchester. His speciality was locomotive and hydraulic machinery design and he patented a revolving box cyclone cotton or jute-baling press. After Nasmyth's Smethurst became a Manchester-based consulting engineer. *PIME*, 1940.

5 Nasmyth Wilson & Co. Ltd., Summary of Shares and Capital, 21 March 1892, TNA, BT31/40370/16751/16.

6 Nasmyth Wilson & Co., Ltd. Summary of Shares and Capital, 24 March 1902, TNA, BT31/40370/16751/27.

7 It is clear from a letterheaded certificate for a boiler that William Maclean Wilson was manager in 1886, SA, U268/B3/1, p.194.

8 *PICE*, vol.131, pp.381-383 and *PIME* (1898), pp.139-140.

9 *EPJ*, 4 February 1921.

10 This compares with £45,488 19s 2d for Robert Wilson senior and £20,633 5s 4d for Robert Wilson junior.

11 The *Manchester Guardian*, 28 May 1946.

12 Greg was certainly working for Nasmyth's on 1 May 1900 when he attended a meeting of the LMA, Minute Book No.2, NRM, 1997/8434/10.

13 Nasmyth Wilson & Co. Ltd., Particulars of Directors, etc., TNA, BT31/40370/16751/97.

14 See note 5.

15 E.H. Greg Jr to E.H. Greg, 26 January 1884, quoted in Rose (1986), pp.92-93.

16 *EPJ*, 29 July 1910.

17 Information from Adam Daber.

18 *PIME* (1900), pp.328-329. For further references see Bell (1975), p.59.

19 *EPJ*, 9 November 1934.

20 *Ibid*, 9 March 1900. This comment referred to local disputes for the workforce were involved in the national strike of 1897-98.

21 British Patent No. 7,152, 13 July 1911, amended 4 March 1912. Bolas later applied his ingenuity to a mechanical race game apparatus with a roulette device facility for determining the relative positions of the race competitors.

22 *EPJ*, 10 May 1907.

23 *The Railway Gazette* (1913), p.

24 *The Ironmonger* (1887), p.61.

25 One of these hammers manufactured for Thomas Walmsley & Sons of Bolton in 1917 now stands preserved on Deane Road, Bolton, outside Bolton Institute of Higher Education.

26 See note 19.

27 See note 22.

28 The levels of demand could vary quite considerably: in 1882, 1893 and 1916 less than ten locomotives were produced whereas more than forty left the factory in 1905, 1907, 1908, 1914, 1915 and 1917.

29 The percentage of locomotives constructed for the main line railways by the railway workshops during the four decades covered by this chapter was 73, 72, 80 and 78. Atkins (1999), p.125.

30 These ranged in price from £1,450 for a locomotive named *Kirkless* for Wigan to £2,525 for the *Ellesmere* delivered to Walkden in 1912.

31 The twelve 0-6-2 tank engines sent to the Taff Vale Railway in 1919 were priced between £6,660 10s 10d and £7,077 4s 2d indicating both the inflation in construction prices that had taken place during the war and the detailed accuracy of the cost accounting systems.

32 The 3ft 6in gauge of the West Carberry Railway, the 3ft gauge of the County Donegal Railway and the 5ft 3in gauge of the Great Northern Railway.

33 One concerned a loss of six-and-a-quarter per cent on a contract worth £11,225 with the Great Northern Railway of Ireland while the other was an eleven per cent loss on an 0-8-0 tank engine delivered to Astley & Tyldesley Colliery for £2,060. The highest profit margin achieved during this decade was five-and-a-half per cent on a contract with the County Donegal Railway.

34 According to an account of 1907, each new locomotive design would require over a hundred drawings which would take between one and two months to complete. This process would obviously add to the cost. *EPJ*, 10 May 1907.

35 It was during this period that Nasmyth's made the change from oval to pyramid-shaped works plates so distinguishing the appearance of its work plates from those of its competitors such as Beyer Peacock, North British and The Vulcan Foundry. The 0-6-2 engine, Works Number 751, delivered to the Corporation of Western Egypt in 1906 was the first Nasmyth engine fitted with the new works plate.

36 A. Godley, Under Secretary of State for India, to Nasmyth Wilson & Co., Ltd. 24 June 1902, SLHL, SN42.

37 E.H. Greg to A.Godley, 1 July 1902, SLHL, SN42.

38 A. Godley to Nasmyth Wilson & Co. Ltd., 21 July 1902, SLHL, SN42.

39 E.H. Greg to Lord Inverforth, 29 March 1921, TNA, MUN 4/6838.

40 *EPJ*, 21 January 1910.

41 Figures derived from Atkins (1999), p.123.

Chapter eight

1 *Morning Post*, 28 November 1928.

2 Mensforth (1981), p.29.

3 Grant (1950), p.66.

4 All the John Brown directors except Spencer have entries in *Who Was Who*. For the latter, see *Halifax Evening Courier*, 8 March 1940. Spencer was chairman of Nasmyth's before being invited to join the Firth Brown board in 1930.

5 *EPJ*, 15 October 1920.

6 *Ibid*, 26 November 1937 and *Journal of the Institution of Locomotive Engineers*, vol.27, no.140 (Nov-Dec 1937).

7 *Journal of the Institution of Locomotive Engineers*, vol.48, no.261 (1958-1959) and the membership and obituary files kept at the Institutions of Mechanical Engineers and Civil Engineers.

8 *Engineering*, vol.120 (3 July 1925), p.15.

9 Donald Manson was the son of a wagon wright. He was educated at Hutcheson's School, Glasgow, and later attended night classes at Glasgow & West of Scotland Technical College where his studies included Applied Maths, 'Steam' and Laboratory and Design for which he was awarded First Class certificates. His practical engineering experience was gained at Dubs & Co where he remained until the firm amalgamated with Sharp Stewart and Neilson Reid to form the North British Locomotive Co. in 1903. At this point Manson moved to Nasmyth's as a draughtsman. He was a devout nonconformist Christian and declined an honour for his work during the First World War in finding accommodation for Belgian refugees. I am grateful to Ian Manson for this information.

10 *Engineering*, vol.139, (Feb 1935), p.191.

11 *Ibid*, vol.147, (March 1939), pp.302–304.

12 *Ibid*, vol.141 (Feb 1936), p.209. By 1937 Germany had supplanted Britain as the principal supplier to Brazil and had destroyed Britain's former monopoly links with her own empire by securing strong footholds in both South Africa and India.

13 *Engineering*, vol.143, (March 1937), p.307.

14 *Ibid*, vol.148, (Sept 1939), pp.259-260.

15 Steam locomotives in use fell from 20,983 (1933) to 19,646 (1938) while electric motor-rail vehicles increased from 1,489 to 1,986 over the same period.

16 Nasmyth Wilson & Co. Ltd., Balance Sheet at 31 December 1921, TNA, BT31/40370/16751/73.

17 *EPJ*, 29 September 1933.

18 When eight of these outsize engines (Works Nos. 1,594–1,601) left the factory in 1930 bound for Manchester Docks for shipment in a fully erected state, the move entailed lowering and slewing the railway line through two tunnels and removing the coping stones from Eccles station platform. The work had to be done between midnight Saturday and midnight Sunday. R. Arbuthnott (1958-59), p.471.

19 LMA Minutes, NRM, 1997/8434/19.

20 Nasmyth Wilson & Co. Ltd., Annual Return, TNA, BT31/40370/16751/106.

21 For a history of the ROF, Patricroft, see Hay (1949), pp.41-43 and Weinbren & Putman (1995).

Bibliography

Arbuthnott, R., 'Presidential Address', *Journal of the Institution of LocomotiveEngineers*, 48 (1958-59) pp.441-474.

Atkins, P., *The Golden Age Of Steam Locomotive Building* (1999).

Baker, A.C. and Civil, T.D.A., *Bagnalls of Stafford* (1973).

Barnabe, G., *Rails Through Majorca* (2003).

Bell, S.P., *A Biographical Index of British Engineers In The 19th Century* (1975).

Bradley, R.P., *Giants of Steam, the full story of the North British Locomotive Co Ltd* (1995).

Burgess, K., *The Origins of British Industrial Relations* (1975).

Campbell, R.H., 'The North British Locomotive Company between the wars' *Business History*, 20 (1978), 201-234.

Cantrell, J.A., 'James Nasmyth and the Bridgewater Foundry: Partners and Partnerships', *Business History*, 23 (1981), 346-358.

Cantrell, J.A., *James Nasmyth and the Bridgewater Foundry. A study of entrepreneurship in the early engineering industry* (1984).

Cantrell, J.A., 'James Nasmyth and the Steam Hammer', *TNS*, 56 (1985), 133-138.

Cantrell, J.A. and Cookson, Gillian (eds.), *Henry Maudslay and the Pioneers of the Machine Age* (2002).

Cantrell, J.A., 'Two Maudslay Protégés: Francis Lewis and George Nasmyth', *TNS*, 73 (2003), 257-274.

Cantrell, J.A., 'The Bridgewater Foundry 1836-1940: the rise and fall of a famous firm', *The Local Historian*, 34 (2004), pp.235-248.

Clark, Sylvia, 'Chorlton Mills and Their Neighbours', *Industrial Archaeology Review*, 2 (1978).

Clarke, J.F., *Power on Land & Sea, a history of R & W Hawthorn Leslie* (1978).

Cooksey, J.C.B., *Alexander Nasmyth 1758-1840: a Man of the Scottish Renaissance* (1991).

Dewhurst, P.C., 'Norris Locomotives in England, 1838-1842', *TNS*, 26 (1947-1949), 13-46.

Dickenson, R., 'James Nasmyth and the Liverpool Iron Trade', *Trans. History Society of Lancs and Cheshire*, 108 (1956).

Dyos, H.J. and Aldcroft, D.H., *British Transport* (1969).

Fleming, A.I.M., McKinstry, S. and Wallace, K., 'The Decline and Fall of the NorthBritish Locomotive Company, 1940-62: Technological and FinancialMismanagement or Institutional Failure?' *Business History*, 42 (2000), 67-90.

Grant, Sir A., *Steel & Ships* (1950).

Hay, I., *R.O.F. The Story of The Royal Ordnance Factories 1939-1948* (1949).

Hills, R.L., *Life and Inventions of Richard Roberts (1789-1864)* (2002).

Hills, R.L. and Patrick, D., *Beyer, Peacock Locomotive Builders to the World* (1982).

Hume, J.R. and Moss, M.S., *Beardmore, the History of a Scottish Industrial Giant* (1979).

The Ironmonger, 'The Engineering and other Industries of Manchester and District', (September, 1887), 60-61.

Kirby, M.W., 'Product Proliferation in the British Locomotive Building Industry, 1850-1914: An Engineer's Paradise?' *Business History*, 30 (1988), 287-305.

Kitson Clark, E., *Kitsons of Leeds 1837-1937* (1938).

The Locomotive Publishing Co., *The Vulcan Locomotive Works* (1930).

Love & Barton, *Manchester As It Is* (1839).

Lowe, J.W., *British Steam Locomotive Builders* (1975).

Marshall, J., *A Biographical Dictionary of Railway Engineers* (1978).

Mensforth, E., *Family Engineers* (1981).

Moore, G.S., *Nasmyth Wilson & Co Ltd* (c.1981).

Musson, A.E. and Robinson, Eric, *Science and Technology in the Industrial Revolution* (1969).

Political & Economic Planning, *Engineering Reports III, Locomotives* (1951).

The Railway Gazette, 'The New Works of Messrs Nasmyth, Wilson & Co Ltd, Patricroft, Manchester'
    (1913), 770-790 and reprinted as a separate supplement with additional illustrations (nd), pp.1-36.

Redman, R.N., *The Railway Foundry, Leeds, 1839-1969: E.B. Wilson-Hudswell Clarke & Co. Ltd* (1972).

Rose, Mary B. *The Gregs of Quarry Bank Mill* (1986).

Rolt, L.T.C., *A Hunslet Hundred* (1964).

Rowlandson, T.S., *History of the Steam Hammer* (1864).

Smiles, S., *Industrial Biography* (1863).

Smiles, S. (ed.), *James Nasmyth, Engineer: An Autobiography* (1883).

Townley, D.H., *The Hunslet Engine Works* (1998).

Wear, R., *Barclay 150 1840-1990* (1990).

Warren, J.G.H., *A Century of Locomotive Building by Robert Stephenson & Co.,
    1823-1923* (1923, reprinted 1970).

Warren, K., *Armstrong's of Elswick* (1989).

Weinbren, D. and Putman, T., *A Short History of Royal Ordnance Patricroft – Nasmyth's
    Bridgewater Foundry* (1995).

Person Index

Locomotives produced at the Bridgewater Foundry 1838-1938

Key

Inside cylinders are denoted by the cylinder dimensions placed in brackets

AR	Assam Railway
BAR	Bengal Assam Railway
BCR	Bengal Central Railway
BkSR	Bikaner State Railway
CR	Central Railway India
EAR & H	East African Railways & Harbours
EBR	Eastern Bengal Railway (Pakistan)
EBS	Eastern Bengal State Railway
ER	Eastern Railway India
GSR	Great Southern Railway Ireland
GWR	Great Western Railway
JNR	Japanese National Railways
JR	Jodhpur (State) Railway
LMSR	London, Midland & Scottish Railway
LNER	London & North Eastern Railway
LYR	Lancashire and Yorkshire Railway
MR	Malayan Railways
MSMR	Madras & Southern Mahratta Railway
MSR	Mysore State Railway
NER	North Eastern Railway India
NGSR	Nizam's Guaranteed State Railway
NR	Northern Railway India
NWR	North Western Railway India
OTR	Oudh Tirhut Railway
Renfe	Spanish National Railways Network
ROD	Railway Operating Dept.
RM	Rail Motor
RSR	Royal State Railway (Thailand)
SER	South Eastern Railway India
SG	Standard Gauge
SR	Southern Railway India
ST	Saddle Tank
SVB	Stockholm Vesteras Berglagens
T	Tank
WR	Western Railway, India

Works No.	Dispatch Date	Type	Cylinders	Driving Wheels	Gauge	Customer	Customer Name or Number
1	1839	2-2-2	(12½ x 16)	5' 0"	SG	Built for stock. Sold to J. Waring, Contractor to Manchester & Birmingham	BRIDGEWATER
2	1839	2-2-0	(12 x 18)	5' 6"	SG	London & Southampton	28 HAWK
3	"	"	"	"	"	"	29 FALCON
4	"	"	"	"	"	"	30 RAVEN
5	1839	0-4-2	(14 x 18)	5' 0"	SG	Manchester & Leeds	7 ROCHDALE > LYR 132
6	"	"	"	"	"	"	8 BRADFORD > LYR 133
7	"	"	"	"	"	"	9 HULL > LYR
8	1840	2-2-2	(14 x 18)	5' 0"	SG	Built for stock. Midland Counties	WOLF > 39
9	1841	2-2-2	(14 x 18)	5' 0"	SG	Built for stock. Darwen Mills	NASMYTH
10	"	"	"	"	"	"	PATRICROFT
11	1840	2-2-0	(12 x 18)	5' 6"	SG	Midland Counties Railway	20 LIGHTNING
12	"	"	"	"	"	"	21 LUCIFER
13	"	"	"	"	"	"	22 HURRICANE
14	"	"	"	"	"	"	23 FIREBRAND
15	"	"	"	"	"	"	24 RAINBOW
16	"	"	"	"	"	"	25 SIROCCO
17	1840	4-2-0	11½ x 20	4' 0"	SG	Birmingham & Gloucester	19 DEFFORD > Midland 280
18	1841	"	"	"	"	"	27 DROITWICH > Midland 284
19							26 ASHCHURCH
20	1841	2-2-2	(14 x 18)	5' 6"	SG	Manchester & Leeds	22 DERBY > LYR
21	"	"	"	"	"	"	23 SHEFFIELD > LYR
22	1841	4-2-0	11½ x 20	4' 0"	SG	Birmingham & Gloucester	28 PERSHORE
23	"	"	"	"	"	"	29 UPTON > Midland 285
24	"	"	"	"	"	"	30 LIFFORD > Midland 286
25	1841	2-2-2	(15 x 18)	7' 0"	7' 0"	Great Western Railway	65 ACHILLES
26	"	"	"	"	"	"	67 MILO
27	"	"	"	"	"	"	71 HECTOR
28	"	"	"	"	"	"	78 CASTOR
29	"	"	"	"	"	"	85 MENTOR
30	"	"	"	"	"	"	107 BELLONA
31	"	"	"	"	"	"	102 ACTAEON
32	"	"	"	"	"	"	103 CENTAUR
33	1841	4-2-0	11½ x 20	5' 6"	SG	Zwilchenbart & Co. for Kaiser Ferdinand Nordbahn, Austria	41 CYCLOPS
34	"	"	"	"	"		42 GOLIATH
35	1842	2-2-2	(15 x 18)	7' 0"	7' 0"	Great Western Railway	111 ORION
36	"	"	"	"	"	"	112 DAMON
37	"	"	"	"	"	"	114 ELECTRA
38	"	"	"	"	"	"	115 PRIAM
39	"	"	"	"	"	"	126 POLLUX
40	"	"	"	"	"	"	132 PHOENIX
41	"	"	"	"	"	"	134 PEGASUS
42	"	"	"	"	"	"	135 STENTOR
43	"	0-6-0	(16 x 24)	5' 0"	"	"	128 HERCULES
44	"	"	"	"	"	"	129 SAMSON
45	"	"	"	"	"	"	130 GOLIATH
46	"	"	"	"	"	"	133 TITYOS
47	1845	2-2-2	15 x 22	5' 6"	SG	R. Stephenson & Co. for Dover Line (South Eastern Railway)	88 rebuilt as 2-4-0 (1848)
48	"	"	"	"	"	"	89 rebuilt as 2-4-0 (1849)
49	"	"	"	"	"	"	90 rebuilt as 2-2-2 Well tank (1848)
50	"	"	"	"	"	"	91 rebuilt as 2-4-0 (1848)
51	1846	"	"	"	"	R. Stephenson & Co. for Paris & Orleans	76 > 64 (1852)
52	"	"	"	"	"	"	77 > 65 (1852)
53	"	"	"	"	"	R. Stephenson & Co. for Dover Line (South Eastern Railway)	92 rebuilt as Crampton engine (1848)
54	"	"	"	"	"	"	93 rebuilt as 2-2-2 Well tank (1848)
55	"	"	"	"	"	"	94 rebuilt as 2-2-2 Well tank (1848)
56	"	2-4-0	(15 x 22)	4' 6"	"	"	95
57	"	"	"	"	"	"	96
58	"	"	"	"	"	"	97
59	"	"	"	"	"	"	98
60	"	"	"	"	"	"	99
61	"	"	"	"	"	"	100
62	1847	2-2-2	15 x 22	5' 6"	"	"	110 rebuilt as 2-4-0 (1849)
63	"	"	"	"	"	"	112 rebuilt as 2-4-0 (1848)
64	"	0-6-0	(15 x 24)	4' 6"	"	R. Stephenson & Co. for London & North Western (Southern Division)	137
65	"	"	"	"	"	"	138
66	"	"	"	"	"	"	139
67	"	"	"	"	"	"	140
68	"	"	"	"	"	"	141
69	"	"	"	"	"	"	142
70	"	"	"	"	"	"	143
71	"	"	"	"	"	"	144
72	"	2-2-2	"	6' 6"	"	R. Stephenson & Co. for York Newcastle & Berwick	161
73	"	"	"	"	"	"	162

Works No.	Dispatch Date	Type	Cylinders	Driving Wheels	Gauge	Customer	Customer Name or Number
74	1847	2-2-2	15 x 20	6' 6"	SG	London & North Western	191 > North Eastern Division 47
75	"	"	"	"	"	"	192 > North Eastern Division 48
76	"	"	"	"	"	"	193 > North Eastern Division 49
77	1848	"	"	"	"	"	194 > North Eastern Division 50
78	"	"	"	"	"	"	195 > North Eastern Division 51
79	"	"	"	"	"	"	196 > North Eastern Division 52
80	1848	0-6-0	(15 X 24)	4' 8"	SG	York Newcastle & Berwick	174
81	"	"	"	"	"	"	175
82	"	"	"	"	"	"	183
83	"	"	"	"	"	"	184
84	"	"	"	"	"	"	191
85	"	"	"	"	"	"	192
86	1849	"	"	"	"	"	193
87	"	"	"	"	"	"	194
88	"	"	"	"	"	"	195
89	"	"	"	"	"	"	196
90	1850	"	"	"	"	"	197
91	"	"	"	"	"	"	198
92	"	"	"	"	"	"	199
93	"	"	"	"	"	"	200
94	"	"	"	"	"	"	201
95	"	"	"	"	"	"	202
96	1851	"	"	"	"	"	203
97	"	"	"	"	"	"	204
98	"	"	"	"	"	"	205
99	"	"	"	"	"	"	206
100	1852	0-6-0	(16½ x 24)	5' 3"	SG	Great Northern Railway	318
101	"	"	"	"	"	"	319
102	"	"	"	"	"	"	320
103	"	"	"	"	"	"	321
104	"	"	"	"	"	"	322
105	"	"	"	"	"	"	323
106	1853	"	"	"	"	"	324
107	"	"	"	"	"	"	325
108	"	"	"	"	"	"	326
109	"	"	"	"	"	"	327
110	1861	0-6-0	(17 x 24)	4' 10"	SG	Kirkless Hall Coal & Iron Co.	
111	1862	0-4-0ST	(10 x 15)	3' 0½"	4' 1½"	"	JUNO
112	"	"	"	"	"	"	MARS
113	"	"	"	"	"	"	VENUS
114	1867	2-2-2	(16 x 22)	6' 6"	SG	London Brighton & South Coast	236 ARUNDEL > 476
115	"	"	(16½ x 22)	"	"	"	237 REIGATE > 477
116	"	"	(16 x 22)	"	"	"	238 SHOREHAM > 478
117	"	"	(16½ x 22)	"	"	"	239 POLEGATE > 479
118	"	"	(16 x 22)	"	"	"	240 ST LEONARDS > 480
119	"	"	(16½ x 22)	"	"	"	241 EASTBOURNE > 481
120	1872	0-6-0	(17 x 24)	5' 1"	"	Great Eastern Railway	507
121	"	"	"	"	"	"	508
122	"	"	"	"	"	"	509
123	"	"	"	"	"	"	510
124	"	"	"	"	"	"	511
125	1873	0-4-4T	11 x 18	3' 6"	Metre	Indian State Railway	B1
126	"	"	"	"	"	"	B2
127	"	"	"	"	"	"	B3
128	"	"	"	"	"	"	B4
129	"	"	"	"	"	"	B5
130	"	"	"	"	"	"	B6
131	"	"	"	"	"	"	B7 > 26 > Burma 119
132	"	"	"	"	"	"	B8
133	"	"	"	"	"	"	B9
134	"	"	"	"	"	"	B10
135	"	"	"	"	"	"	B11
136	"	"	"	"	"	"	B12
137	"	"	"	"	"	"	B13
138	"	"	"	"	"	"	B14
139	"	"	"	"	"	"	B15
140	"	"	"	"	"	"	B16
141	"	"	"	"	"	"	B17
142	1874	"	"	"	"	"	B18
143	"	"	"	"	"	"	B19 > 54
144	"	"	"	"	"	"	B20 > 55 > Burma 120
145	1873	0-6-0T	14 x 20	3' 0"	SG	Nora Karlskoga, Sweden	4 CARLSDAHL
146	"	"	"	"	"	"	5 BOFORS
147	"	"	"	"	"	"	6 STRIBERGET
148	1874	0-6-4T	13½ x 20	3' 0"	Metre	Indian State Railway	C1

Works No.	Dispatch Date	Type	Cylinders	Driving Wheels	Gauge	Customer	Customer Name or Number
149	1874	0-6-4T	13½ x 20	3' 0	Metre	Indian State Railway	C2
150	"	"	"	"	"	"	C3
151	"	"	"	"	"	"	C4
152	"	"	"	"	"	"	C5
153	"	"	"	"	"	"	C6
154	"	"	"	"	"	"	C7
155	"	"	"	"	"	"	C8
156	"	"	"	"	"	"	C9
157	"	"	"	"	"	"	C10
158	"	"	"	"	"	"	C11
159	"	"	"	"	"	"	C12
160	"	"	"	"	"	"	C13
161	"	"	"	"	"	"	C14
162	"	"	"	"	"	"	C15
163	"	"	"	"	"	"	C16
164	"	"	"	"	"	"	C17
165	"	"	"	"	"	"	C18
166	"	"	"	"	"	"	C19
167	"	"	"	"	"	"	C20
168	1874	0-6-0ST	(16 x 24)	4' 7"	SG	Rhymney, Wales	33 > GWR 659
169	"	"	"	"	"	"	34
170	"	"	"	"	"	"	35
171	"	"	"	"	"	"	36 > GWR 660
172	"	"	"	"	"	"	37
173	"	"	"	"	"	"	38
174	1874	4-4-0T	(11 x 18)	3' 6"	3' 0"	Majorca Railway	1 MALLORCA
175	"	"	"	"	"	"	2 PALMA
176	"	"	"	"	"	"	3 INCA
177	1875	0-6-0ST	15 x 24	3' 6"	SG	Nora Karlskoga, Sweden	7 NORA > Swedish Govt 289
178	1875	0-4-2T	(9 x 14)	2' 6"	Metre	Indian State, N.W. Provinces	A1 > E. Indian Rly Collieries
179	"	"	"	"	"	"	A2
180	"	"	"	"	"	"	A3
181	"	"	"	"	"	"	A4
182	"	"	"	"	"	"	A5 > E. Indian Rly Collieries
183	"	"	"	"	"	"	A6
184	1875	0-4-0WT	9 x 14	2' 6"	SG	Manchester Corporation Gas Works	M/C Electricity Dept 2
185	1876	0-6-0T	14 x 22	3' 3"	SG	Nora Karlskoga, Sweden	8
186	"	"	"	"	"	"	9
187	"	"	"	"	"	"	10
188	1876	0-6-0T	13 x 18	3' 6"	3' 0"	Majorca Railway	4 MANACOR
189	"	"	"	"	"	"	5 FELANITX
190	1876	0-6-0	(19 x 26)	5' 0"	5' 6"	Valencia, Spain	> N. Spain 1707 > Renfe 030 2451
191	"	"	"	"	"	"	> N. Spain 1708 > Renfe 030 2452
192	"	"	"	"	"	"	> N. Spain 1709 > Renfe 030 2453
193	"	"	"	"	"	"	> N. Spain 1710 > Renfe 030 2454
194	1877	4-4-0T	13 x 18	3' 6"	3' 0"	Majorca Railway	6 SINEU
195	"	"	"	"	"	"	7 LA PUEBLA
196	"	"	"	"	"	"	8 SANTA MARIA
197	"	"	"	"	"	"	9 BINISALEM
198	1878	0-6-0T	13 x 18	3' 0"	SG	Mount Keira Colliery New South Wales	No 1 KEIRA
199	"	"	"	"	"	"	No 2 KEMBLA
200	1878	0-6-0	(19 x 26)	5' 0"	5' 6"	Valencia, Spain	> N. Spain 1711 > Renfe 030 2455
201	"	"	"	"	"	"	> N. Spain 1712 > Renfe 030 2456
202	"	2-4-0	(17½ x 26)	6' 6"	"	"	17 > N. Spain 297
203	"	"	"	"	"	"	18 > N. Spain 298
204	"	"	"	"	"	"	19 > N. Spain 299 > Renfe 120 2081
205	1881	4-4-0T	13½ x 19	3' 6"	3' 0"	Majorca Railway	10 MURO
206	"	"	"	"	"	"	11 PETRA > 18
207	1881	0-6-0T	(17 x 24)	4' 0"	SG	J.Lancaster, Blaina & Nantyglo Iron Co	JOHN O' GAUNT
208	1881	0-6-0T	13 x 20	3' 0"	3' 6"	Tal Tal Railway, Chile	1
209	"	"	"	"	"	"	2
210	"	"	"	"	"	"	3
211	"	"	"	"	"	"	4
212	"	"	"	"	"	"	5
213	"	"	"	"	"	"	6
214	"	"	"	"	"	"	7
215	"	"	"	"	"	"	8
216	1882	4-4-0	16 x 24	5' 0½"	5' 6"	Bengal Central Railway	1 > Eastern Bengal 81 > BCR 18 > EBSR143
217	"	"	"	"	"	"	2 > NGSR 10
218	1883	"	"	"	"	"	3 > Eastern Bengal 82 > BCR 19 > EBSR 144
219	"	"	"	"	"	"	4 > Eastern Bengal 83 > BCR 20 > EBSR 145
220	"	"	"	"	"	"	5 > NGSR 11

Works No.	Dispatch Date	Type	Cylinders	Driving Wheels	Gauge	Customer	Customer Name or Number
221	1883	4-4-0	16 x 24	5' 0½	5' 6"	Bengal Central Railway	6 > Eastern Bengal 84 > BCR 21
222	"	"	"	"	"	"	7 > Eastern Bengal 85 > BCR 22 > EBSR 14(
223	"	"	"	"	"	"	8 > Eastern Bengal 86 > BCR 23 > EBSR 14?
224	1882	0-6-4T	14½ x 20	3' 0"	3' 0"	La Guaira & Caracas, Venezuela	1
225	1883	"	"	"	"	"	2
226	"	"	"	"	"	"	3
227	"	"	"	"	"	"	4
228	"	"	"	"	"	"	5
229	"	"	"	"	"	"	6
230	1883	0-4-0 Tram	10 x 14	2' 6"	Metre	Sharp Stewart & Co.	Probably SS & Co 3093 for Spain
231	"	"	"	"	"	"	Probably SS & Co 3094 for Spain
232	1883	0-6-4T	(16 x 24)	4' 1½"	5' 3"	San Paulo, Brazil	1
233	"	"	"	"	"	"	23 > 14
234	"	"	"	"	"	"	24
235	1883	2-6-0T	13 x 20	3' 6"	Metre	Donna Theresa Christina, Brazil	3 DOM PEDRO II
236	"	"	"	"	"	"	4 DONNA THEREZA
237	"	"	"	"	"	"	5 PRINCEZA
238	"	"	"	"	"	"	6 SANTA CATHERINA
239	"	"	"	"	"	"	7 TIBUAO
240	"	"	"	"	"	"	8 LAGUNA
241	1884	2-6-0	14½ x 18	3' 5"	3' 6"	Brazilian Imperial Central Bahia	
242	"	"	"	"	"	"	
243	"	"	"	"	"	"	
244	"	"	"	"	"	"	
245	"	"	"	"	"	"	
246	"	"	"	"	"	"	
247	"	"	"	"	"	"	
248	"	"	"	"	"	"	
249	1884	0-6-0T	(17 x 24)	4' 0"	SG	John Lancaster & Co	LANCASTER
250	1884	4-4-0T	12 x 18	3' 6"	Metre	Sorocabana Companhia, Brazil	
251	"	"	"	"	"	"	
252	1884	2-6-2	15 x 20	4' 1"	3' 6"	NZ Govt. Hurunui-Bluff	V 136
253	"	"	"	"	"	"	V 132
254	"	"	"	"	"	"	V 128
255	"	"	"	"	"	"	V 127
256	"	"	"	"	"	"	V 114
257	"	"	"	"	"	"	V 125
258	"	"	"	"	"	"	V 129
259	"	"	"	"	"	"	V 35
260	"	"	"	"	"	"	V 63
261	"	"	"	"	"	"	V 126
262	1884	2-6-0	13 x 17	3' 0"	Metre	Santa Fé, Argentina	SANTA FÉ
263	"	"	"	"	"	"	SAN CARLOS
264	"	4-4-0	12 x 16	3' 3"	"	"	SIMON DE TRIANDO
265	"	"	"	"	"	"	ROCA
266	"	"	"	"	"	"	GONZALES
267	1884	2-6-0	13 x 17	3' 3"	Metre	Bahia & San Francisco, Brazil	1
268	"	"	"	"	"	"	2
269	"	"	"	"	"	"	3
270	1885	4-4-0	"	3' 6"	"	"	4
271	"	"	"	"	"	"	5
272	1885	2-8-0	15 x 20	3' 5"	3' 6"	NZ Govt. Auckland	P 51 > P 268
273	"	"	"	"	"	"	P 52 > P 269
274	1885	2-8-0	15 x 20	3' 5"	3' 6"	NZ Govt. Hurunui-Bluff	P 134
275	"	"	"	"	"	"	P 135
276	1885	2-8-0	15 x 20	3' 5"	3' 6"	NZ Govt. Auckland	P 53 > P 270
277	1885	2-8-0	15 x 20	3' 5"	3' 6"	NZ Govt. Hurunui-Bluff	P 52
278	"	"	"	"	"	"	P 107
279	"	"	"	"	"	"	P 60
280	"	"	"	"	"	"	P 133
281	"	"	"	"	"	"	P 25
282	1885	2-6-2	15 x 20	4' 1"	3' 6"	NZ Govt. Wellington & Manawatu	6 > V 450
283	"	"	"	"	"	"	7 > V 451
284	"	"	"	"	"	"	8 > V 452
285	1884	0-6-4T	14½ x 20	3' 0"	3' 0"	La Guaira & Caracas, Venezuela	7
286	"	"	"	"	"	"	8
287	1885	4-6-0	13 x 17	3' 0"	Metre	Santa Fé Extension, Argentina	6
288	"	"	"	"	"	"	7
289	"	"	"	"	"	"	8
290	"	"	"	"	"	"	9
291	1886	4-4-0	12 x 16	4' 0"	"	"	10
292	"	"	"	"	"	"	11
293	"	"	"	"	"	"	12
294	"	"	"	"	"	"	13
295	"	"	"	"	"	"	14

Works No.	Dispatch Date	Type	Cylinders	Driving Wheels	Gauge	Customer	Customer Name or Number
96	1885	2-6-2T	14 x 20	3' 4"	3' 0"	Caracus-Antimano, Venezuela	1 CARACAS
97	"	"	"	"	"	"	2 ANTIMANO
98	1885	0-6-0T	13 x 18	3' 0"	3' 6"	Imperial, Japan	59 > Nippon 22 > JNR 1106
99	1886	0-6-0T	(17 x 24)	4' 0"	SG	Blaina & Nantyglo Iron Co.	HUGH MASON
00	1886	2-4-2T	13½ x 20	4' 4"	3' 6"	Imperial, Japan	69 > Nippon 18 > JNR 400
01	"	"	"	"	"	"	71 > Nippon 19 > JNR 401
02	"	"	"	"	"	"	73 > Nippon 20 > JNR 403
03	"	"	"	"	"	"	75 > Nippon 21 > JNR 402
04	1886	0-6-0T	14 x 22	3' 5"	SG	Ince Coal & Canal Co.	GIDLOW > Chatterley Whitfield Colly ROGER
05	1886	0-6-0T	13 x 18	3' 0"	3' 6"	Imperial, Japan	77 > 55 > JNR 1100
06	"	"	"	"	"	"	79 > 57 > JNR 1101
07	"	"	"	"	"	"	81 > Nippon 23 > JNR 1107
08	"	"	"	"	"	"	83 > 60 > Taiwan 9
09	"	"	"	"	"	"	85 > Nippon 24 > JNR 1108
10	"	"	"	"	"	"	87 > 63 > JNR 1102
11	1887	4-4-0T	12 x 18	3' 9"	3' 6"	Midland, NZ	1 > NZ Govt. 310
12	"	"	"	"	"	"	5 > NZ Govt. 314
13	1887	4-4-0T	12 x 18	3' 9"	3' 6"	Delagoa Bay & East African	1 PRINCE LUIZ PHILIPPE
14	"	"	"	"	"	"	2 PAUL KRUGER
15	1887	4-4-0T	12 x 18	3' 9"	3' 6"	Midland, NZ	2 > NZ Govt. 311
16	1887	4-4-0T	12 x 18	3' 6"	Metre	Sorocabana Companhia, Brazil	
17	"	"	"	"	"	"	
18	"	"	"	"	"	"	
19	"	"	"	"	"	"	
20	1887	4-6-0T	15 x 20	3' 3"	3' 0	Majorca Railway	12 SAN JUAN
21	"	"	"	"	"	"	13 LLOSETA
22	1887	4-4-0T	12 x 18	3' 9"	3' 6"	Midland, NZ	3 > NZ Govt. 312
23	"	"	"	"	"	"	4 > NZ Govt. 313
24	1887	4-6-0T	14 x 20	3' 9"	3' 6"	Delagoa Bay & East African	3 > Oliphants Fontein Brick & Tile Co. (1908)
25	"	"	"	"	"	"	4
26	1887	2-4-2T	14 x 20	4' 4"	3' 6"	Imperial, Japan	82 > 59 > 850 > 661
27	"	"	"	"	"	"	84 > 61 > 851 > 662 > Kojaku 6
28	"	"	"	"	"	"	109 > Nippon 31 > JNR 602
29	"	"	"	"	"	"	111 > Nippon 32 > JNR 603
30	"	"	"	"	"	"	113 > Nippon 33 > JNR 604
31	"	"	"	"	"	"	115 > Nippon 34 > JNR 605
32	"	"	"	"	"	"	117 > Nippon 35 > JNR 606
33	1888	"	"	"	"	"	119 > Nippon 36 > JNR 607
34	"	"	"	"	"	"	121 > 85 > 854 > 665 > Kojaku 12
35	"	"	"	"	"	"	123 > 87 > 885 > 666 > Hanwa 666
36	"	2-6-2T	16 x 22	4' 0"	"	"	102 > 74 > 3080
37	"	"	"	"	"	"	104 > 76 > 3081
38	1888	0-6-0T	13 x 18	3' 0"	3' 6"	Sanyo > Hokkaido Coal Mining	18 > JNR 1113
39	"	"	"	"	"	"	17 > JNR 1112
40	"	"	"	"	"	Sanyo > Imperial, Japan	9 > 190 > 124 > 1104
41	1888	4-4-0T	12 x 18	3' 4"	3' 6"	West Carberry	Schull & Skibbereen No. 4 ERIN > GSR 48
42	1888	2-4-2T	14 x 20	4' 4"	3' 6"	Imperial, Japan	137 > Nippon 40 > JNR 608
43	"	"	"	"	"	"	139 >Nippon 41 > JNR 609
44	"	"	"	"	"	"	141 > Kobu 1 > JNR 622 > Yabaket 7
45	"	"	"	"	"	"	143 > Kobu 2 > JNR 623
46	"	"	"	"	"	"	86 > 62 > 852 > 663 > Kojaku 7
47	"	"	"	"	"	"	88 > 64 > 853 > 664
48	1888	4-4-0T	12 x 18	3' 6"	Metre	Sorocabana Companhia, Brazil	17
49	"	"	"	"	"	"	18
50	"	"	"	"	"	"	19
51	"	"	"	"	"	"	20
52	1888	0-6-0T	12 x 18	3' 0"	3' 0"	Interoceanic	25
53	"	"	"	"	"	"	26
54	1889	4-6-0	15 x 20	3' 0"	3' 6"	Queensland Govt.	205
55	"	"	"	"	"	"	206
56	"	"	"	"	"	"	207
57	"	"	"	"	"	"	208
58	"	"	"	"	"	"	209
59	"	"	"	"	"	"	210
60	"	"	"	"	"	"	211
61	"	"	"	"	"	"	212
62	"	"	"	"	"	"	213
63	"	"	"	"	"	"	214
64	"	"	"	"	"	"	215
65	"	"	"	"	"	"	216
66	"	"	"	"	"	"	217
67	"	"	"	"	"	"	218
68	"	"	"	"	"	"	219
369	1889	2-6-0T+T	16 x 22	4' 0"	3' 6"	Imperial, Japan	138 > Nippon 54 > JNR 7600

Works No.	Dispatch Date	Type	Cylinders	Driving Wheels	Gauge	Customer	Customer Name or Number
370	1889	2-6-2T+T	16 x 22	4' 0"	3' 6"	Imperial, Japan	140 > Nippon 55 > JNR 7601
371	"	"	"	"	"	"	142 > Nippon 56 > JNR 7602
372	1890	"	"	"	"	"	144 > Nippon 57 > JNR 7603
373	"	"	"	"	"	"	146 > Nippon 58 > JNR 7604
374	"	"	"	"	"	"	148 > Nippon 59 > JNR 7605
375	1889	2-8-0	18 x 26	4' 0"	SG	Mexican Pacific	
376	"	"	"	"	"	"	
377	1890	"	"	"	"	"	> SVB 51
378	"	"	"	"	"	"	> SVB 52
379	"	"	"	"	"	"	> SVB 53
380	"	"	"	"	"	"	> SVB 54
381	"	"	"	"	"	"	> SVB 55
382	"	"	"	"	"	"	> SVB 56
383	1890	2-4-2T	14 x 20	4' 4"	3' 6"	Imperial, Japan	157 > Nippon 42 > 603 > Kojaku 11
384	"	"	"	"	"	"	159 > Nippon 43 > 611
385	"	"	"	"	"	"	161 > Nippon 44 > 612 > Kojaku 5
386	"	"	"	"	"	"	163 > Nippon 45 > 613
387	"	"	"	"	"	"	165 > Nippon 46 > 614
388	"	"	"	"	"	"	167 > Nippon 47 > 615
389	1889	0-4-0T	10 x 14	2' 6"	3' 0"	Majorca Tramway	2 > Majorca Rly 6, MARRATXI
390	1890	2-4-2T	14 x 20	4' 4"	3' 6"	Imperial, Japan	169 > 856 > 667
391	"	"	"	"	"	"	171 > 857 > 668
392	"	"	"	"	"	"	173 > 858 > 669
393	"	"	"	"	"	"	175 > 859 > 670
394	"	"	"	"	"	"	177 > 860 > 671
395	"	"	"	"	"	"	179 > 861 > 672
396	"	"	"	"	"	"	183 > Nippon 53 > 621
397	"	"	"	"	"	"	185 > Nippon 48 > 616
398	"	"	"	"	"	"	187 > Nippon 49 > 617
399	"	"	"	"	"	"	189 > Nippon 50 > 618
400	"	"	"	"	"	"	191 > Nippon 51 > 619
401	"	"	"	"	"	"	181 > Nippon 52 > 620 > Chugika 13
402	1890	0-6-2T	15½ x 20	3' 0"	3' 0"	La Guaira & Caracas, Venezuela	13
403	"	"	"	"	"	"	14
404	Cancelled						
405	"						
406	"						
407	1891	0-6-2T	15½ x 20	3' 0"	3' 0"	La Guaira & Caracas, Venezuela	15
408	"	"	"	"	"	"	16
409	1891	2-6-0	17 x 24	4' 6"	5' 5¾"	Pontevedra-Carril (>West Galicia)	6 > Oeste 541 > Renfe 130.2011
410	"	"	"	"	"	"	7 > Oeste 542 > Renfe 130.2012
411	1891	0-6-0ST	15 x 22	3' 9"	5' 5¾"	Triano, Spain	14 MUSQUES > Renfe 030.0228
412	Cancelled						
413	"						
414	1891	4-6-0T	15 x 20	3' 3"	3' 0"	Majorca Railway	14 MARRATZI
415	"	"	"	"	"	"	15 ALARO
416	1891	4-4-0T	13 x 18	3' 6"	Metre	Luchana & Munguia, Spain	2 MUNGUIA > 7 Bilbao Suburban 2
417	1891	0-6-4T	16 x 20	3' 1½"	3' 0"	Mexican Southern	11
418	"	"	"	"	"	"	12
419	"	"	"	"	"	"	13 F. BULNES
420	"	"	"	"	"	"	14
421	1891	0-6-2T	15½ x 20	3' 0"	3' 0"	La Guaira & Caracas, Venezuela	17
422	"	"	"	"	"	"	18
423	1891	4-4-0	14 x 20	4' 7⅛"	3' 6"	Beira & Mashonaland	3 (completed 1897)
424	"	"	"	"	"	"	4 (completed 1897)
425	1892	4-4-2T	17 x 26	6' 1"	SG	London, Tilbury & Southend	31 ST PANCRAS > Midland 2140
426	"	"	"	"	"	"	32 LEYTON > Midland 2141
427	"	"	"	"	"	"	33 WANSTEAD > Midland 2142
428	"	"	"	"	"	"	34 TOTTENHAM > Midland 2143
429	"	"	"	"	"	"	35 WEST HAM > Midland 2144
430	"	"	"	"	"	"	36 WALTHAMSTOW > Midland 2145
431	1892	0-4-0T	10 x 14	2' 6"	2' 7½"	Somorrostro Iron Ore Co., Spain	
432	"		11 x 16	2' 9"	"	"	
433	1892	2-4-0T	15 x 20	4' 6"	5' 5½"	Bilbao & Portugalete	8 ZORROZA > Renfe 120.0221
434	"	"	"	"	"	"	9 LUCHANA > Renfe 120.0222
435	1892	2-6-0T	14½ x 21	3' 6"	Metre	Elgoibar & San Sebastian, Spain	> Vascongados 105 YGARTUA
436	"	"	"	"	"	"	
437	"	"	"	"	"	"	
438	"	"	"	"	"	"	
439	"	"	"	"	"	"	
440	"	"	"	"	"	"	
441	1892	0-6-0ST	12½ x 18	3' 0"	3' 6"	Broken Hill Proprietary Co., NSW	No. 1 LITTLE BESSIE
442	1893	0-6-0ST	(16 x 20)	4' 3½"	SG	Wigan Coal & Iron Co.	KIRKLESS
443	1893	2-4-0T	15 x 20	4' 6"	5' 5½"	Bilbao & Portugalete	10 OLAVEACA
444	"	"	"	"	"	"	11 CANTALOJAS

Works No.	Dispatch Date	Type	Cylinders	Driving Wheels	Gauge	Customer	Customer Name or Number
445	1893	0-4-0ST	12 x 18	3' 0"	SG	Bury Corporation	ELTON
446	1893	2-4-2T	14 x 20	4' 4"	3' 6"	Sobu, Japan	1 > JNR 628
447	"	"	"	"	"	"	2 > JNR 629
448	1894	"	"	"	"	"	3 > JNR 630 > Kojaku 9
449	1894	2-4-2T	14 x 20	4' 4"	3' 6"	Sangu, Japan	1 > JNR 651
450	1894	2-4-2T	14 x 20	4' 4"	3' 6"	Kobu, Japan	4 > JNR 624
451	"	"	"	"	"	"	5 > JNR 625
452	1894	2-4-2T	14 x 20	4' 4"	3' 6"	Sangu, Japan	2 > JNR 652
453	"	"	"	"	"	"	3 > JNR 653
454	1894	0-4-0ST	14 x 20	3' 3½"	SG	Brown Bayley's Steel Co., Sheffield	4
455	1894	2-6-0T	14½ x 21	3' 6"	Metre	Elgoibar & San Sebastian, Spain	
456	1894	2-6-0T	14½ x 20	3' 6"	Metre	Bilbao & Durango, Spain	> Vascongados 104 AURRERA
457	1894	2-4-2T	14 x 20	4' 4"	3' 6"	Sobu, Japan	5 > JNR 632
458	1894	0-6-0T	13 x 18	3' 0"	3' 6"	Kioto, Japan	> Taiwan
459	"	"	"	"	"	"	No.1
460	1895	0-4-4T	(17 x 24)	5' 3"	SG	Cambrian Railway	3 > GWR 10
461	"	"	"	"	"	"	5 > GWR (11)
462	"	"	"	"	"	"	7 > GWR (15)
463	1895	2-4-0T	15 x 20	4' 6"	5' 5⅞"	Bilbao & Portugalete	No.12 > No. 1 (4/1907)
464	1895	0-6-4T	14 x 20	3' 0"	750mm	Alhamilla Railway	3 LUCAINENA
465	"	"	"	"	"	"	4 NIJAR
466	"	"	"	"	"	"	5 AGUA AMARGA
467	1895	2-4-2T	14 x 20	4' 4"	3' 6"	Bosco, Japan	1 > Ganetsu > Nippon 18 > JNR 600 > Iwaki Cement
468	"	"	"	"	"	"	2 > Ganetsu > Nippon 19 > JNR 601
469	"	"	"	"	"	"	3 > JNR 631
470	1895	4-4-0	13 x 17	3' 6"	Metre	Bahia & San Francisco, Brazil	6
471	1895	0-6-0T	13 x 18	3' 0"	3' 6"	M. Brunker & Co. for Imperial, Japan	180 > 1103
472	1896	2-4-2T	14 x 20	4' 4"	3' 6"	Sobu, Japan	6 > JNR 633
473	"	"	"	"	"	"	7 > JNR 634
474	"	"	"	"	"	"	8 > JNR 635
475	"	"	"	"	"	"	9 > JNR 636 > Mitsui Coal Co. (Hokkaido) No. 2
476	"	"	"	"	"	"	10 > JNR 637
477	"	"	"	"	"	"	11 > JNR 638
478	1896	0-6-0T	14 x 18	3' 0"	3' 6"	Sanuki, Japan	5 > Sanyo 136 > JNR 1200
479	"	"	"	"	"	"	6 > Sanyo 137 > JNR 1201
480	"	"	"	"	"	"	7 > Sanyo 138 > JNR 1202 > Mutsu 3 > JNR 1730
481	"	"	"	"	"	"	8 > Sanyo 139 > JNR 1203
482	1896	0-6-0T	13 x 18	3' 0"	3' 6"	Hokuyetsu, Japan	1 > JNR 1109
483	"	"	"	"	"	"	2 > JNR 1110
484	1896	2-4-2T	14 x 20	4' 4"	3' 6"	Narita, Japan	1 > JNR 674
485	"	"	"	"	"	"	2 > JNR 675
486	"	"	"	"	"	"	3 > JNR 677 > Hanwa
487	"	"	"	"	"	"	4 > JNR 676
488	1896	0-6-0T	13 x 18	3' 0"	3' 6"	Chiuyetsu, Japan	1 > JNR 1050
489	"	"	"	"	"	"	2 > JNR 1051
490	"	"	"	"	"	"	3 > JNR 1052 > AOMI Electric
491	1896	2-4-2T	14 x 20	4' 4"	3' 6"	Kobu, Japan	8 > JNR 626 > Minato 6
492	"	"	"	"	"	"	9 > JNR 627
493	1896	2-4-2T	14 x 20	4' 4"	3' 6"	Seibu Kawagoe, Japan	3
494	1896	0-6-0T	14 x 18	3' 0"	3' 6"	Nanao, Japan	1 > JNR 1206
495	"	"	"	"	"	"	2 > JNR 1207
496	"	"	"	"	"	"	3 > JNR 1208
497	1896	2-4-2T	14 x 20	4' 4"	3' 6"	Sangu, Japan	4 > JNR 654
498	"	2-4-0T	12 x 18	4' 0"	"	"	5 > Tobu 57 > Hitachi Wks No. 1 > JNR 100
499	1896	0-6-0T	14 x 18	3' 0"	3' 6"	Kanto, Japan	> Sobu 13 > JNR 1205
500	"	"	"	"	"	"	> Sobu 12 > JNR 1204
501	1897	0-6-0T	13 x 18	3' 0"	3' 6"	Toyokawa, Japan	1 > JNR 1280
502	"	"	"	"	"	"	2 > JNR 1281
503	"	"	"	"	"	"	3 > Nagoya 13
504	1897	2-4-0T	15 x 20	4' 6"	5' 5⅞"	Triano, Spain	17 > Renfe 120.0211
505	1897	2-4-2T	14½ x 20	3' 1"	3' 6"	Kansei, Japan	21 > JNR 870
506	"	"	"	"	"	"	22 > JNR 871
507	1897	2-4-2T	14 x 20	4' 4"	3' 6"	Boso, Japan	5 > JNR 646
508	1897	2-4-2T	14 x 20	4' 4"	3' 6"	Chugoku, Japan	101 > JNR 660
509	"	"	"	"	"	"	67 > JNR 656 > Shimabara No. 1
510	"	"	"	"	"	"	68 > JNR 657
511	"	"	"	"	"	"	69 > JNR 658
512	"	"	"	"	"	"	70 > JNR 659
513	1897	0-6-0T	13 x 18	3' 0"	3' 6"	Chugokee, Japan	2 > JNR 1221
514	"	"	"	"	"	"	4 > JNR 1223
515	"	"	"	"	"	"	3 > JNR 1222
516	1897	2-4-2T	14 x 20	4' 4"	3' 6"	Osaka, Japan	18 > Kansei 69 > JNR 648

Works No.	Dispatch Date	Type	Cylinders	Driving Wheels	Gauge	Customer	Customer Name or Number
517	1897	2-4-2T	14 x 20	4' 4"	3' 6"	Osaka, Japan	19 > Kansei 70 > JNR 649
518	"	"	"	"	"	"	20 > Kansei 71 > JNR 650
519	1898	2-4-2T	13½ x 20	4' 4"	3' 6"	Omi, Japan	1
520	"	"	"	"	"	"	2
521	1898	2-4-2T	13½ x 20	4' 4"	3' 6"	Chugokee, Japan	1 > JNR 490
522	1898	0-6-0T	13 x 18	3' 0"	3' 6"	Kanan, Japan	1 > Osaka 1
523	"	"	"	"	"	"	2 > Osaka 2
524	1898	0-6-0T	13 x 18	3' 0"	3' 6"	Nippon, Japan	21 > JNR 1105
525	1897	0-4-0T	11 x 16	2' 9"	800mm	Somorrostro Iron Ore Co., Spain	Union Mines (7/1909)
526	1898	4-4-0T	13½ x 19	3' 6"	3' 0"	Majorca Railway	16 PORRERAS
527	"	"	"	"	"	"	17 MONTNIRE
528	1898	2-4-2T	14 x 20	4' 4"	3' 6"	Bisai, Japan	> JNR 673
529	"	"	"	"	"	"	> JNR 639
530	"	"	"	"	"	"	> JNR 643
531	1898	0-6-0T	15 x 22	4' 0"	3' 6"	Hokuyetsu, Japan	8 > JNR 1940
532	"	"	"	"	"	"	9 > JNR 1941
533	"	"	"	"	"	"	10 > JNR 1942
534	"	"	"	"	"	"	11 > JNR 1943
535	"	"	"	"	"	"	12 > JNR 1944
536	1898	0-6-0T	13 x 18	3' 0"	3' 6"	Daigoku Dobokukantokusa, Japan	
537	"	"	"	"	"	"	
538	"	"	"	"	"	"	
539	"	"	"	"	"	"	
540	"	"	"	"	"	"	
541	"	"	"	"	"	"	
542	1898	2-4-2T	14½ x 20	4' 4"	3' 6"	Kansei, Japan	46 > JNR 872
543	"	"	"	"	"	"	47 > JNR 873
544	"	"	"	"	"	"	48 > JNR 874
545	"	"	"	"	"	"	49 > JNR 875
546	"	"	"	"	"	"	50 > JNR 876
547	"	"	"	"	"	"	51 > JNR 877
548	1898	0-6-0ST	(16 x 20)	4' 3½"	SG	Wigan Coal & Iron Co.	WANTAGE
549	1898	4-4-0	13 x 17	3' 6"	Metre	Bahia & San Francisco, Brazil	7
550	1898	2-6-0T	14½ x 21	3' 6"	Metre	Bilbao & Durango, Spain	> Vasco Navarro BL13 VIZCAYA
551	"	"	"	"	"	"	
552	1899	0-6-0	(18 x 26)	4' 8"	SG	Furness Railway	7 > LMSR 12468
553	"	"	"	"	"	"	8 > LMSR 12469
554	"	"	"	"	"	"	9 > LMSR 12470
555	"	"	"	"	"	"	10 > LMSR 12471
556	"	"	"	"	"	"	11 > LMSR 12472
557	"	"	"	"	"	"	12 > LMSR 12473
558	1899	0-4-4T	(17 x 24)	5' 3"	SG	Cambrian Railway	8 > GWR 19
559	"	"	"	"	"	"	9 > GWR 20
560	"	"	"	"	"	"	23 > GWR 21
561	1899	0-6-0ST	(17 x 24)	4' 7"	SG	Neath & Brecon	7 > GWR 2174
562	"	"	"	"	"	"	8 > GWR 2175
563	1899	2-6-0	15 x 20	3' 4½"	3' 0"	Santa Martha, Columbia	7
564	1899	0-6-0	14 x 20	3' 6½"	Metre	Indian State, Jodhpur Bikaner	013 > JR 013 > NR 13
565	"	"	"	"	"	"	014 > JR 014 > NR 14 > 36004
566	"	"	"	"	"	"	015 > JR 015 > NR 15
567	"	"	"	"	"	"	016 > JR 016 > NR 16
568	"	"	"	"	"	"	017 > JR 017 > NR 17 > 36005
569	"	"	"	"	"	"	018 > JR 018 > NR 18 > 36006
570	"	"	"	"	"	"	019 > JR 019 > NR 19 > 36010
571	1900	"	"	"	"	"	020 > JR 020 > NR 20 > 36007
572	"	"	"	"	"	"	021 > JR 021 > NR 21 > 36008
573	"	"	"	"	"	"	022 > JR 022 > NR 22
574	"	"	"	"	"	"	023 > JR 023 > NR 23 > 36009
575	"	"	"	"	"	"	024 > JR 024 > NR 24
576	"	"	"	"	"	"	025 > Mesopotania 262
577	"	"	"	"	"	"	026 > Mesopotania 263
578	1900	0-6-4T	16½ x 20	3' 1½"	3' 6"	Costa Rica	33
579	"	2-6-0	"	3' 4½"	"	"	50
580	"	"	"	"	"	"	51
581	1900	4-4-0T	14½ x 20	4' 0"	Metre	Elgoibar & San Sebastian, Spain	
582	"	"	"	"	"	"	
583	"	"	"	"	"	"	
584	1900	0-6-0ST	(17 x 24)	4' 7½"	SG	Brecon & Merthyr	27 > GWR 2171
585	"	"	"	"	"	"	28 > GWR 2172
586	"	"	"	"	"	"	29 > GWR 2173
587	1900	0-6-0T	13½ x 18	3' 0"	3' 6"	Hokkaido, Japan	2 > JNR 1170
588	1900	0-6-0	(18 x 26)	5' 0"	SG	North Staffordshire	159 > LMSR 2351 > 8673
589	"	"	"	"	"	"	160 > LMSR 2352 > 8674
590	"	"	"	"	"	"	161 > LMSR 2353 > 8675
591	"	"	"	"	"	"	162 > LMSR 2354 > 8676

Works No.	Dispatch Date	Type	Cylinders	Driving Wheels	Gauge	Customer	Customer Name or Number
592	1900	0-6-0	(18 x 26)	5' 0"	SG	North Staffordshire	163 > LMSR 2355 > 8677
593	"	"	"	"	"	"	164 > LMSR 2356 > 8678
594	1900	0-6-0ST	(16 x 20)	4' 3½"	SG	Wigan Coal & Iron Co.	JUPITER
595	1900	0-6-0T	14 x 18	3' 0¼"	3' 6"	Nankai, Japan	20 > Fuji Seitetsu
596	"	"	"	"	"	"	21 > Amagasaki Seitetsu > JNR 1360
597	"	"	"	"	"	"	22 > Musishing
598	1901	0-6-0T	15 x 22	4' 6"	3' 6"	Hokuyetsu, Japan	16 > JNR 2080
599	"	"	"	"	"	"	17 > JNR 2081
600	1901	4-4-4T	15½ x 21	4' 1½"	3' 6"	Western Australian Government	1
601	"	"	"	"	"	"	19
602	"	"	"	"	"	"	20
603	"	"	"	"	"	"	25
604	"	"	"	"	"	"	26
605	"	"	"	"	"	"	27
606	"	"	"	"	"	"	132
607	"	"	"	"	"	"	256
608	"	"	"	"	"	"	257
609	"	"	"	"	"	"	258
610	"	"	"	"	"	"	259
611	"	"	"	"	"	"	260
612	"	"	"	"	"	"	261
613	"	"	"	"	"	"	262
614	"	"	"	"	"	"	263
615	1901	2-4-2T	14 x 20	4' 4"	3' 6"	Sobu, Japan	> Hokkaido 5 > JNR 647
616	1901	2-6-0	16 x 20	3' 4½"	3' 6"	Costa Rica	54
617	"	"	"	"	"	"	55
618	1901	2-4-2T	14 x 20	4' 4"	3' 6"	Sangu, Japan	6 > JNR 655
619	1901	2-4-2T	14½ x 20	4' 6"	3' 6"	Kansei, Japan	72 > JNR 878
620	"	"	"	"	"	"	73 > JNR 879
621	1901	4-4-0T	14½ x 21	4' 0"	Metre	Bilbao & Durango, Spain	
622	"	"	"	"	"	"	
623	"	"	"	"	"	"	
624	"	"	"	"	"	"	
625	1901	2-4-2T	14 x 20	4' 1"	3' 6"	Imperial Taiwan	18
626	"	"	"	"	"	"	19
627	"	"	"	"	"	"	20
628	"	"	"	"	"	"	21
629	"	"	"	"	"	"	22
630	1902	"	"	"	"	"	23
631	"	"	"	"	"	"	24
632	"	"	"	"	"	"	25
633	"	"	"	"	"	"	26
634	"	"	"	"	"	"	27
635	1902	2-4-2T	14½ x 20	4' 6"	3' 6"	Kansei, Japan	74 > JNR 880
636	"	"	"	"	"	"	75 > JNR 881
637	"	"	"	"	"	"	76 > JNR 882
638	"	"	"	"	"	"	77 > JNR 883
639	1902	2-4-2T	14 x 20	4' 4"	3' 6"	Kobu, Japan	> Kawague 4
640	1902	0-4-0ST	12 x 18	3' 0"	SG	Bury Corporation	BURY
641	1902	4-6-2	17 x 23	4' 6"	3' 6"	Western Australian Government	291
642	"	"	"	"	"	"	292
643	"	"	"	"	"	"	293
644	"	"	"	"	"	"	294
645	"	"	"	"	"	"	295
646	"	"	"	"	"	"	296
647	"	"	"	"	"	"	297
648	"	"	"	"	"	"	298
649	"	"	"	"	"	"	299
650	"	"	"	"	"	"	300
651	"	"	"	"	"	"	301
652	"	"	"	"	"	"	302
653	"	"	"	"	"	"	303
654	"	"	"	"	"	"	304
655	"	"	"	"	"	"	305
656	1902	0-6-0ST	(16 x 20)	4' 3½"	SG	Wigan Coal & Iron Co.	SULTAN
657	1902	0-4-0T	11 x 16	2' 9"	800mm	Somorrostro Iron Ore Co., Spain	
658	1903	2-4-2	13 x 20	3' 6½"	Metre	Indian State, Bikaner Bhatinda	038 > 049 > BkSR 10
659	"	"	"	"	"	"	039 > 050 > BkSR 11
660	"	"	"	"	"	"	040 > 051 > BkSR 12
661	"	"	"	"	"	"	041 > 052 > BkSR 13
662	1903	0-6-0	14 x 20	3' 6½"	Metre	Eastern Bengal, Northern	79 > 579
663	"	"	"	"	"	"	80 > 580
664	"	"	"	"	"	"	81 > 581 > Mesopotamia 255
665	"	"	"	"	"	Eastern Bengal, Dacca	23 > EBSR 85 > 585
666	"	"	"	"	"	"	24 > EBSR 86 > 586

Works No.	Dispatch Date	Type	Cylinders	Driving Wheels	Gauge	Customer	Customer Name or Number
667	1903	0–6–0	14 x 20	3' 6½"	Metre	Eastern Bengal, Dacca	25 > EBSR 87 > 587
668	"	4–4–0	"	4' 5"	"	Eastern Bengal, Northern	109 > 620
669	"	"	"	"	"	"	110 > 621
670	"	"	"	"	"	"	111 > 622
671	"	"	"	"	"	"	112 > 623
672	"	"	"	"	"	"	113 > 624
673	"	"	"	"	"	"	114 > 625
674	1903	2–4–2T	14 x 20	4' 4"	3' 6"	Kyoto, Japan	6 > JNR 644
675	"	0–6–0T	13 x 18	3' 0"	"	Toyokawa, Japan	4 > Bantan No. 1 > Toshiba Shikama Works No. 1
676	"	0–6–4T	12 x 16	3' 0½"	2' 5½"	Delta, Egypt	75
677	"	"	"	"	"	"	76
678	"	"	"	"	"	"	77
679	"	"	"	"	"	"	78
680	"	"	"	"	"	"	79
681	"	"	"	"	"	"	80
682	"	"	"	"	"	"	81
683	"	"	"	"	"	"	82
684	"	"	"	"	"	"	83
685	"	"	"	"	"	"	84
686	"	"	"	"	"	"	85
687	"	"	"	"	"	"	86
688	1903	2–4–2T	14 x 20	4' 4"	3' 6"	Kyoto, Japan	7 > JNR 645
689	1904	0–6–2T	(18 x 26)	5' 1"	SG	Furness Railway	98 > LMSR 11625
690	"	"	"	"	"	"	99 > LMSR 11626
691	"	"	"	"	"	"	100 > LMSR 11627
692	"	"	"	"	"	"	101 > LMSR 11628
693	"	"	"	"	"	"	102 > LMSR 11629
694	1904	2–4–2T	14 x 20	4' 5"	3' 6"	Sobu, Japan	22 > JNR 640
695	"	"	"	"	"	"	23 > JNR 641
696	"	"	"	"	"	"	24 > JNR 642
697	1904	4–6–4T	15 x 21	3' 9"	3' 0"	County Donegal Joint Committee	12 ESKE > 9
698	"	"	"	"	"	"	13 OWENEA > 10
699	"	"	"	"	"	"	14 ERNE > 11
700	"	"	"	"	"	"	15 MOURNE > 12
701	1904	0–4–0ST	14 x 20	4' 1"	5' 6"	East Indian Railway	1/980 Construction Locomotives
702	"	"	"	"	"	"	2/980 "
703	"	"	"	"	"	"	3/980 "
704	"	"	"	"	"	"	4/980 "
705	"	"	"	"	"	"	5/980 "
706	"	"	"	"	"	"	6/980 "
707	1904	4–4–0	10 x 15	3' 4½"	2' 6"	Cyprus Govt.	11
708	"	"	"	"	"	"	12
709	"	2–6–0	"	2' 3½"	"	"	21
710	"	"	"	"	"	"	22
711	1905	0–6–4T	12 x 16	3' 0½"	2' 5½"	Delta, Egypt	87
712	"	"	"	"	"	"	88
713	"	"	"	"	"	"	89
714	"	"	"	"	"	"	90
715	"	"	"	"	"	"	91
716	"	"	"	"	"	"	92
717	1905	4-6-0 P Class	15½ x 22	4' 9"	Metre	Bengal & North Western	226 > OTR 226 > NER 701
718	"	"	"	"	"	"	227 > OTR 227 > NER 709 > 31542
719	"	"	"	"	"	"	228 > OTR 228 > NER 710 > 31543
720	"	"	"	"	"	"	229 > OTR 229 > NER 711 > 31544
721	"	"	"	"	"	"	230 > OTR 230
722	"	"	"	"	"	"	231 > OTR 231 > NER 712 > 31545
723	"	"	"	"	"	"	232 > OTR 232 > NER 713 > 31546
724	"	"	"	"	"	"	233 > OTR 233 > NER 714 > 31547
725	"	"	"	"	"	"	234 > OTR 234 > NER 715 > 31548
726	"	"	"	"	"	"	235 > OTR 235 > NER 702 > 31535
727	"	"	"	"	"	"	236 > OTR 236 > NER 716 > 31549
728	"	"	"	"	"	"	237 > OTR 237 > NER 717 > 31550
729	"	"	"	"	"	"	238 > OTR 238 > NER 718 > 31551
730	"	"	"	"	"	"	239 > OTR 239 > NER 719 > 31552
731	"	"	"	"	"	"	240 > OTR 240 > NER 720 > 31553
732	"	"	"	"	"	"	241 > OTR 241 > NER 721 > 31554
733	1905	4-6-0 P Class	15½ x 22	4' 9"	Metre	Eastern Bengal Railway	134 > 13 > BAR 13 > EBR (Pakistan) 13
734	"	"	"	"	"	"	135 > 14 > BAR 14 > AR 14 > NER 813 > 31671
735	"	"	"	"	"	"	136 > 15 > BAR 15 > AR 15 > NER 814 > 31672
736	"	"	"	"	"	"	137 > 16 > BAR 16 > EBR (Pakistan) 16
737	"	"	"	"	"	"	138 > 17 > BAR 17 > AR 17 > NER 815 > 31673

Works No.	Dispatch Date	Type	Cylinders	Driving Wheels	Gauge	Customer	Customer Name or Number
738	1905	4-6-0 R Class	15 x 22	4' 0"	Metre	Eastern Bengal Railway	160 > 201 > BAR 201 > AR 201 > NER 532 > 31804
739	"	"	"	"	"	"	161 > 202 > Iraq 160
740	"	"	"	"	"	"	162 > 203 > BAR 203 > AR 203 > NER 533 > 31805
741	"	"	"	"	"	"	163 > 204 > BAR 204 > AR 204 > NER 534 > 31806
742	"	"	"	"	"	"	164 > 205 > EBR (Pakistan) 205
743	"	"	"	"	"	"	165 > 206 > EBR (Pakistan) 206
744	"	"	"	"	"	"	166 > 207 > EBR (Pakistan) 207
745	"	"	"	"	"	"	167 > 208 > EBR (Pakistan) 208
746	"	"	"	"	"	"	168 > 209 > EBR (Pakistan) 209
747	"	"	"	"	"	"	169 > 210 > BAR 210 > AR 210 > NER 535 > 31807
748	1905	0-4-0ST	14 x 20	4' 1"	5' 6"	East Indian Railway	7/85 Construction Locomotives
749	"	"	"	"	"	"	8/85 "
750	"	"	"	"	"	"	9/85 "
751	1906	0-6-2	14 x 20	3' 0"	2' 5½"	Corporation of Western Egypt	751 > 2751
752	"	"	"	"	"	"	752 > 2752
753	"	"	"	"	"	"	753
754	1906	4-6-0	15½ x 22	4' 9"	Metre	Bengal & North Western	242 > OTR 242 > NER 703 > 31536
755	"	"	"	"	"	"	243 > OTR 243 > NER 704 > 31537
756	"	"	"	"	"	"	244 > OTR 244 > NER 722 > 31555
757	"	"	"	"	"	"	245 > OTR 245 > NER 723
758	"	"	"	"	"	"	246 > OTR 246 > NER 724 > 31556
759	"	"	"	"	"	"	247 > OTR 247 > NER 725
760	"	"	"	"	"	"	248 > OTR 248 > NER 726 > 31557
761	"	"	"	"	"	"	249 > OTR 249 > NER 727 > 31558
762	"	"	"	"	"	"	250 > OTR 250 > NER 705 > 31538
763	"	"	"	"	"	"	251 > OTR 251 > NER 728 > 31559
764	"	"	"	"	"	"	252 > OTR 252 > NER 706 > 31539
765	"	"	"	"	"	"	253 > OTR 253 > NER 729
766	1906	4-6-0	15 x 22	4' 0"	Metre	Burma Railway	266
767	"	"	"	"	"	"	267
768	"	"	"	"	"	"	268
769	"	"	"	"	"	"	269
770	"	"	"	"	"	"	270
771	"	"	"	"	"	"	271
772	"	"	"	"	"	"	272
773	"	"	"	"	"	"	273
774	"	"	"	"	"	"	274
775	"	"	"	"	"	"	275
776	"	"	"	"	"	"	276
777	"	"	"	"	"	"	277
778	"	"	"	"	"	"	278
779	"	"	"	"	"	"	279
780	"	"	"	"	"	"	280
781	1906	4-4-0T	14 x 20	2' 3¼"	SG	Trinidad Govt.	16
782	1906	0-6-0ST	(17 x 24)	4' 1"	SG	Earl of Ellesmere's Colliery	MADGE
783	1906	4-6-0	15 x 22	4' 0"	Metre	Eastern Bengal Railway	170 > 211 > BAR 211 > AR 211 > NER 536 > 31808
784	"	"	"	"	"	"	171 > 212
785	"	"	"	"	"	"	172 > 213 > BAR 213 > AR 213 > NER 537 > 31809
786	"	"	"	"	"	"	173 > 214 > EBR (Pakistan) 214
787	"	"	"	"	"	"	174 > 215
788	"	"	"	"	"	"	175 > 216 > EBR (Pakistan) 216
789	1907	2-4-2T	14 x 20	4' 5"	3' 6"	Tobu, Japan	9
790	"	"	"	"	"	"	10
791	"	"	"	"	"	"	11
792	"	"	"	"	"	"	12
793	"	"	"	"	"	"	13
794	1907	0-4-0 RM	(9 x 14)	3' 7"	5' 6"	East Indian Railway	1350
795	"	"	"	"	"	"	1351
796	"	"	"	"	"	"	1352
797	"	"	"	"	"	"	1353
798	"	"	"	"	"	"	1354
799	1907	2-6-2T	10 x 15	2' 3½"	2' 6"	Cyprus Govt.	31
800	1907	2-6-2T	17 x 24	4' 4"	5' 6"	Buenos Aires Gt. Southern	289 > 3401
801	"	"	"	"	"	"	290 > 3402
802	"	"	"	"	"	"	291 > 3403
803	"	"	"	"	"	"	292 > 3404
804	"	"	"	"	"	"	293 > 3405
805	"	"	"	"	"	"	294 > 3406
806	"	"	"	"	"	"	295 > 3407

Works No.	Dispatch Date	Type	Cylinders	Driving Wheels	Gauge	Customer	Customer Name or Number
807	1907	2-6-2T	17 x 24	4' 4"	5' 6"	Buenos Aires Gt. Southern	296 > 3408
808	"	"	"	"	"	"	297 > 3409
809	"	"	"	"	"	"	298 > 3410
810	1907	4-6-0	15 x 22	4' 0"	Metre	Eastern Bengal Railway	35 (Dacca) > 191 > 232 > Iraq 162
811	"	"	"	"	"	"	36 (Dacca) > 192 > 233 > EBR (Pakistan) 233
812	"	"	"	"	"	"	37 (Dacca) > 193 > 234 > EBR (Pakistan) 234
813	"	"	"	"	"	"	176 > 217 > Iraq 161
814	"	"	"	"	"	"	177 > 218 > EBR (Pakistan) 218
815	"	"	"	"	"	"	178 > 219
816	"	"	"	"	"	"	179 > 220 > EBR (Pakistan) 220
817	"	"	"	"	"	"	180 > 221 > BAR 221 > AR 221> NER 538 > 31810
818	"	"	"	"	"	"	181 > 222
819	"	"	"	"	"	"	182 > 223
820	"	"	"	"	"	"	183 > 224 > BAR 224 > AR 224 > NER 539 > 31811
821	"	"	"	"	"	"	184 > 225 > EBR (Pakistan) 225
822	"	"	"	"	"	"	185 > 226 > EBR (Pakistan) 226
823	"	"	"	"	"	"	186 > 227 > EBR (Pakistan) 227
824	"	"	"	"	"	"	187 > 228 > EBR (Pakistan) 228
825	"	"	"	"	"	"	188 > 229 > EBR (Pakistan) 229
826	"	"	"	"	"	"	189 > 230 > BAR 230 > AR 230 > NER 540 > 31812
827	"	"	"	"	"	"	190 > 231 > EBR (Pakistan) 231
828	1907	2-6-4T	14 x 21	4' 0"	3' 0"	County Donegal	16 DONEGAL > 4 MEENGLAS
829	"	"	"	"	"	"	17 GLENTIS > 5 DRUMBOE
830	1908	"	"	"	"	"	18 KILLYBEGS > 6 COLUMBKILLE
831	"	"	"	"	"	"	19 LETTERKENNY > 7 FINN
832	"	"	"	"	"	"	20 RAPHOE > 8 FOYLE
833	1908	4-6-2	15½ x 24	4' 6"	Metre	Johore State, India	7 > Fed. Malay States 131
834	"	"	"	"	"	"	8 > Fed. Malay States 132
835	"	"	"	"	"	"	9 > Fed. Malay States 103 > 113
836	"	"	"	"	"	"	10 > Fed. Malay States 104 > 114
837	"	"	"	"	"	"	11 > Fed. Malay States 133
838	"	"	"	"	"	"	12 > Fed. Malay States 134
839	1908	4-6-2	15½ x 24	4' 6"	Metre	Federated Malay States	79
840	"	"	"	"	"	"	80
841	"	"	"	"	"	"	81
842	"	"	"	"	"	"	82
843	1908	0-4-0 RM	11 x 16	3' 3"	Metre	Burma Railway	331
844	"	"	"	"	"	"	332
845	"	"	"	"	"	"	333
846	"	"	"	"	"	"	334
847	1908	2-4-2T	14 x 20	4' 5"	3' 6"	Mitsui & Co., Tobu, Japan	16
848	"	"	"	"	"	"	17
849	"	"	"	"	"	"	18 > Tagawa 14
850	"	"	"	"	"	"	19
851	1908	2-6-2T	10 x 15	2' 3½"	2' 6"	Cyprus Govt.	32
852	1908	0-6-0ST	(17 x 24)	4' 1"	SG	Earl of Ellesmere's Colliery	VIOLET
853	1908	0-6-0T	11 x 16	2' 9"	Metre	Silla a Cullera, Spain	7
854	1908	4-6-0	15 x 22	4' 0"	Metre	Eastern Bengal Railway	194 > 235 > EBR (Pakistan) 235
855	"	"	"	"	"	"	195 > 236 > EBR (Pakistan) 236
856	"	"	"	"	"	"	196 > 237 > EBR (Pakistan) 237
857	"	"	"	"	"	"	197 > 238 > BAR 238 > AR 238 > NER 541 > 31813
858	"	"	"	"	"	"	198 > 239 > BAR 239 > AR 239 > NER 542 > 31814
859	"	"	"	"	"	"	199 > 240 > EBR (Pakistan) 240
860	"	"	"	"	"	"	200 > 241 > EBR (Pakistan) 241
861	"	"	"	"	"	"	201 > 242 > BAR 242 > AR 242 > NER 543 > 31815
862	"	"	"	"	"	"	202 > 243 > BAR 243 > AR 243 > NER 544 > 31816
863	"	"	"	"	"	"	203 > 244 > Iraq 163
864	1908	4-8-0	16 x 22	3' 7"	Metre	Assam Rly & Trading Co.	130 > ABR 126 > BAR 126
865	"	"	"	"	"	"	131 > ABR 127 > BAR 127 > EBR (Pakistan) 127
866	"	"	"	"	"	"	132 > ABR 128 > BAR 128 > AR 128 > NER 933 > 31792
867	"	"	"	"	"	"	133 > ABR 129 > BAR 129 > EBR (Pakistan) 129
868	"	"	"	"	"	"	134 > ABR 130 > BAR 130

Works No.	Dispatch Date	Type	Cylinders	Driving Wheels	Gauge	Customer	Customer Name or Number
9	1908	4-8-0	16 x 22	3' 7"	Metre	Assam Rly & Trading Co.	135 > ABR 131 > BAR 131 > AR 131 > NER 934 > 31793
0	"	2-6-2T	15 x 22	"	"	"	70 > BAR 70 > AR 70
1	"	"	"	"	"	"	71 > BAR 71 > AR 71
2	"	"	"	"	"	"	72 > BAR 72 > AR 72
3	"	"	"	"	"	Assam Bengal	73 > BAR 73 > EBR (Pakistan) 73
4	"	"	"	"	"	"	74 > BAR 74 > EBR (Pakistan) 74
5	"	"	"	"	"	"	75 > BAR 75 > EBR (Pakistan) 75
6	1909	2-6-2T	15 x 22	3' 7"	Metre	Burma Railway	335
7	"	"	"	"	"	"	336
8	"	"	"	"	"	"	337
9	1909	2-6-2	15 x 20	3' 4"	3' 6"	Baro Kano, Nigeria	13 ZOMBA > N207
0	"	"	"	"	"	"	14 LEMU > N208
1	1909	2-6-2	15 x 20	4' 0"	3' 6"	Southern Nigerian	201
2	"	"	"	"	"	"	202
3	"	"	"	"	"	"	203
4	"	"	"	"	"	"	204
5	"	"	"	"	"	"	205
6	"	"	"	"	"	"	206
7	1909	4-6-0	15 x 22	4' 0"	Metre	Madras & Southern Mahratta, India	158 > Iraq 157
8	"	"	"	"	"	"	159
9	"	"	"	"	"	"	160
0	"	"	"	"	"	"	229 > MSR 71 > 61 > SR 31232
1	"	"	"	"	"	"	230 > MSR 72 > 62 > SR 31233
2	"	"	"	"	"	"	231 > MSR 73 > 63 > SR 31234
3	"	"	"	"	"	"	232 > MSR 74 > 64 > SR 31235
4	1909	4-4-0	14 x 20	4' 5"	Metre	Morvi State, India	5 > 15 > 4 > Saurashtra 138 > WR 138
5	"	"	"	"	"	"	6 > 16 > Mesopotamia 01
6	1909	4-6-0	15 x 22	4' 0"	Metre	Madras & Southern Mahratta, India	180 > Mesopotamia 144
7	"	"	"	"	"	"	351 > Mesopotamia 145
8	"	"	"	"	"	"	233 > MSR 75 > 65 > SR 31236
9	"	"	"	"	"	"	234 > MSR 76 > 66 > SR 31237
0	"	"	"	"	"	"	235 > MSR 77 > 67 > SR 31238
1	"	"	"	"	"	"	236 > MSR 78 > 68 > SR 31239
2	"	"	"	"	"	"	237 > MSR 79 > 69
3	1909	4-6-0	15 x 22	4' 0"	Metre	Jodhpur-Bikaner, India	048 > 059 > JR 059
4	"	"	"	"	"	"	049 > 060 > JR 060
5	"	"	"	"	"	"	050 > 061 > JR 061
6	"	"	"	"	"	"	051 > 062 > BkSR 41 > NR 41 > 31429
7	1909	4-4-0	14 x 20	4' 5"	Metre	Morvi State, India	7 > 17 > Saurashtra 139 > WR 139
8	1910	0-4-0 Petrol	5¼ x 6	2' 6"	2' 6"	"	
9	1910	4-6-0	15 x 22	4' 0"	Metre	Jodhpur-Bikaner, India	056 > 063 > BkSR 42 > NR 42 > 31430
0	"	"	"	"	"	"	057 > 064 > BkSR 43 > NR 43 > 31431
1	1910	4-6-0	16 x 22	4' 0"	Metre	Buenos Aires Midland, Brazil	38
2	1910	0-6-0ST	(18 x 26)	4' 3"	SG	Earl of Ellesmere's Colliery	BRACKLEY
3	1910	4-8-0	13 x 16	2' 4"	2' 6"	Sierra Leone Govt.	151
4	"	"	"	"	"	"	152
5	1910	4-6-0	15 x 22	4' 0"	Metre	Madras & Southern Mahratta, India	352
6	"	"	"	"	"	"	353
7	"	"	"	"	"	"	354 > Mesopotamia 146
8	1910	0-8-0T	17 x 23	3' 6"	SG	Astley & Tyldesley Colliery	MADEN
9	1910	4-6-0	15 x 22	4' 0"	Metre	Assam Rly & Trading Co.	31 > BAR 336 > AR 336 > NER 601 > 31825
0	"	"	"	"	"	"	32 > BAR 337 > AR 337 > NER 602 > 31826
1	"	"	"	"	"	"	33 > BAR 338 > AR 338 > NER 603 > 31827
2	"	"	"	"	"	"	34 > BAR 339 > AR 339 > NER 604 > 31828
3	1910	4-6-0	15 x 22	4' 0"	Metre	Burma Railway	346
4	"	"	"	"	"	"	347
5	"	"	"	"	"	"	348
6	1911	2-6-2T	"	3' 7"	"	"	349
7	"	"	"	"	"	"	350
8	"	"	"	"	"	"	351
9	1911	0-6-0	(18 x 26)	4' 7½"	4' 7½"	Gt. Northern of Ireland	9 KELLS
0	"	"	"	"	"	"	109 MOIRA
1	"	"	"	"	"	"	112 KEADY
2	"	"	"	"	"	"	38 KESH
3	"	"	"	"	"	"	39 BERAGH
4	1911	4-6-0	15 x 22	4' 0"	Metre	Burma Railway	352
5	"	"	"	"	"	"	353
6	"	"	"	"	"	"	354
7	"	2-6-2T	"	3' 7"	"	"	355
8	"	"	"	"	"	"	356
9	"	"	"	"	"	"	357
0	"	"	"	"	"	"	358
1	1911	4-8-0	18 x 23	3' 6¾"	3' 6"	Southern Nigerian	255 > 217 (1933)
2	"	"	"	"	"	"	256 > 218 (1933)

Works No.	Dispatch Date	Type	Cylinders	Driving Wheels	Gauge	Customer	Customer Name or Number
943	1911	4-6-0T	15 x 20	3' 3"	3' 0"	Majorca Railway	20 ALGAIDA > 18 > 11
944	"	"	"	"	"	"	21 SANTA EUGENIA > 10
945	1911	4-4-0	(18½ x 26)	6' 2"	5' 6"	Eastern Bengal State	265 > 406 > BAR 406 > EBR (Pakistan) 406
946	"	"	"	"	"	"	266 > 407 > BAR 407 > EBR (Pakistan) 407
947	"	"	"	"	"	"	267 > 408 > BAR 408 > EBR (Pakistan) 408
948	1911	2-6-0	10 x 15	2' 3½"	2' 6"	Cyprus Govt.	23
949	1911	2-6-2	14 x 20	3' 0"	2' 5½"	Western Oasis, Egypt	949
950	1911	0-6-0	(18½ x 26)	4' 7¼"	5' 3"	Gt. Northern Railway of Ireland	165 NEWBLISS
951	1911	2-8-0	20 x 26	4' 6"	5' 6"	East Indian Railway	990 > ER 26694
952	"	"	"	"	"	"	991 > ER 26695
953	"	"	"	"	"	"	992 > NR 2092 > 27141
954	1912	"	"	"	"	"	993 > ER 26680
955	"	"	"	"	"	"	994 > ER 26696
956	1912	2-6-4T	15½ x 21	4' 0"	3' 0"	County Donegal	2A STRABANE > 2 BLANCHE
957	"	"	"	"	"	"	3A STRANORLAR > 3 LYDIA
958	"	"	"	"	"	"	21 BALLYSHANNON > 1 ALICE
959	1912	4-4-0	14 x 20	4' 5"	Metre	Jodhpur-Bikaner, India	060 > 044 > BkSR 76 > NR 76 > 31522
960	"	"	"	"	"	"	061 > 045 > BkSR 77 > NR 77 > 31523
961	"	"	"	"	"	"	062 > 046 > BkSR 78 > NR 78 > 31524
962	"	"	"	"	"	"	063 > 047 > BkSR 79 > NR 79 > 31525
963	"	"	"	"	"	"	064 > 048 > BkSR 80 > NR 80 > 31526
964	"	"	"	"	"	"	058 > 042 > BkSR 75 > NR 75 > 31521
965	"	"	"	"	"	"	059 > 043 > JR 038 > NR 38 > 31530
966	1912	4-8-0	18 x 23	3' 6¾"	3' 6"	Nigerian Railway	257
967	"	"	"	"	"	"	258
968	"	"	"	"	"	"	259
969	1912	2-6-2T	15 x 22	3' 7"	Metre	Burma Railway	374
970	"	"	"	"	"	"	375
971	"	"	"	"	"	"	376
972	"	"	"	"	"	"	377
973	"	"	"	"	"	"	378
974	"	"	"	"	"	"	379
975	"	"	"	"	"	"	380
976	1912	0-6-0ST	(18 x 26)	4' 3"	SG	Earl of Ellesmere's Colliery	ELLESMERE
977	1912	4-6-0	15½ x 22	4' 9"	Metre	Rohilkund & Kumaon, India	75 > OTR 675 > NER 757 > 31587
978	"	"	"	"	"	"	76 > OTR 676 > NER 758 > 31588
979	"	"	"	"	"	"	77 > OTR 677 > NER 759
980	1912	2-6-2T	15 x 22	3' 7"	Metre	Uganda Railway	81 > 381
981	"	"	"	"	"	"	82 > 382
982	"	"	"	"	"	"	83 > 383
983	1913	4-6-0	15 x 22	4' 0"	Metre	Jodhpur-Bikaner, India	065 > JR 065
984	"	"	"	"	"	"	066 > JR 066
985	"	"	"	"	"	"	067 > JR 067
986	"	"	"	"	"	"	068 > JR 068
987	"	"	"	"	"	"	069 > JR 069
988	"	"	"	"	"	"	075 > 070 > BkSR 44 > NR 44 > 31432
989	"	"	"	"	"	"	076 > 071 > BkSR 45 > NR 45 > 31433
990	"	"	"	4' 9"	"	"	070 > 0115 > JR 0115 > NR 115 > 31449
991	"	"	"	"	"	"	071 > 0116 > JR 0116 > NR 116 > 31450
992	"	"	"	"	"	"	072 > 0117 > JR 0117 > NR 117 > 31451
993	"	"	"	"	"	"	073 > 0118 > JR 0118 > NR 118 > 31452
994	"	"	"	"	"	"	074 > 0119 > JR 0119
995	1913	2-6-0T	18 x 26	4' 8½"	5' 6"	Bombay Port Trust	1 > Indian Iron & Steel Co. Ltd.
996	"	"	"	"	"	"	2 > "
997	"	"	"	"	"	"	3 > "
998	"	"	"	"	"	"	4 > "
999	"	"	"	"	"	"	5 > "
1000	"	"	"	"	"	"	6 > "
1001	1913	4-8-0	13 x 16	2' 4"	2' 6"	Sierra Leone	153
1002	"	"	"	"	"	"	154
1003	"	"	"	"	"	"	155
1004	"	"	"	"	"	"	156
1005	1913	4-6-0	18 x 22	4' 6"	3' 6"	Nigerian Railway	401 > 460 rebuilt as 4-6-2T 17½ x 22
1006	"	"	"	"	"	"	402 > 461 "
1007	"	"	"	"	"	"	403 > 462 "
1008	"	"	"	"	"	"	404 > 463 "
1009	1913	2-6-4T	15 x 22	3' 7"	Metre	Uganda Railway	91 > 391 > EAR & H 1001
1010	"	"	"	"	"	"	92 > 392 > EAR & H 1002
1011	"	"	"	"	"	"	93 > 393 > EAR & H 1003
1012	"	"	"	"	"	"	94 > 394 > EAR & H 1004
1013	"	"	"	"	"	"	95 > 395 > EAR & H 1005
1014	1913	2-8-2	14½ x 18	2' 10"	2' 6"	Bengal Nagpur, India	0066 > NWR 73
1015	"	"	"	"	"	"	0067
1016	"	"	"	"	"	"	0068
1017	"	"	"	"	"	"	0069 > SER 658

Works No.	Dispatch Date	Type	Cylinders	Driving Wheels	Gauge	Customer	Customer Name or Number
018	1913	2-8-2	14½ x 18	2' 10"	2' 6"	Bengal Nagpur, India	0070 > NWR 74
019	"	"	"	"	"	"	0071 > SER 612
020	"	"	"	"	"	"	0072 > NWR 53
021	"	"	"	"	"	"	0073 > NWR 54
022	1914	"	"	"	"	"	0074 > SER 610
023	"	"	"	"	"	"	0075 > SER 611
024	1914	4-8-0	18 x 23	3' 6¾"	3' 6"	Nigerian Railway	260
025	"	"	"	"	"	"	261
026	1914	2-6-4T	(18½ x 26)	5' 1½"	5' 6"	East indian Railway	159
027	"	"	"	"	"	"	160 > ER 26821
028	"	"	"	"	"	"	161 > ER 26822
029	"	"	"	"	"	"	162 > ER 26823
030	"	"	"	"	"	"	163 > ER 26824
031	"	"	"	"	"	"	164 > ER 26825
032	1914	2-6-0T	18 x 26	4' 8½"	5' 6"	Bombay Port Trust	7 > Indian Iron & Steel Co.
033	"	"	"	"	"	"	8 > "
034	1914	4-8-0	16 x 22	3' 7"	Metre	Uganda Railway	121
035	"	"	"	"	"	"	122
036	"	"	"	"	"	"	123
037	"	"	"	"	"	"	124
038	"	"	"	"	"	"	125
039	"	"	"	"	"	"	126
040	"	"	"	"	"	"	127
041	"	2-6-4T	15 x 22	"	"	"	96 > 396 > EAR & H 1006
042	"	"	"	"	"	"	97 > 397 > EAR & H 1007
043	"	"	"	"	"	"	98 > 398 > EAR & H 1008
044	1914	4-8-0	16 x 22	3' 7"	Metre	Nizams Guaranteed State, India	181 > Iraq 228
045	"	"	"	"	"	"	182 > Iraq 229
046	"	"	"	"	"	"	183
047	"	"	"	"	"	"	184 > Iraq 230
048	"	"	"	"	"	"	185 > AR
049	"	"	"	"	"	"	186 > AR
050	"	"	"	"	"	"	187 > AR
051	"	"	"	"	"	"	188 > Iraq 231
052	"	"	"	"	"	"	189 > Iraq 232
053	"	"	"	"	"	"	190 > Iraq 233
054	1914	0-6-0T	18 x 24	4' 0"	5' 6"	East Indian Railway	677 > ER 34364
055	"	"	"	"	"	"	678 > ER 34365
056	"	"	"	"	"	"	679 > ER 34366
057	"	"	"	"	"	"	680 > ER 34367
058	"	"	"	"	"	"	681 > ER 34368
059	"	"	"	"	"	"	682 > ER 34369
060	1914	4-6-4T	15 x 22	3' 6½"	3' 6"	South African	341
061	"	"	"	"	"	"	342
062	"	"	"	"	"	"	343
063	"	"	"	"	"	"	344
064	"	"	"	"	"	"	345
065	1915	"	"	"	"	"	346
066	1915	4-6-0	16½ x 22	4' 9"	Metre	Eastern Bengal State	249 > 35 > BAR 35 > EBR (Pakistan) 35
067	"	"	"	"	"	"	250 > 36 > BAR 36 > AR 36 > NER 823 > 31688
068	"	"	"	"	"	"	251 > 37 > BAR 37 > EBR (Pakistan) 37
069	"	"	"	"	"	"	252 > 38 > BAR 38 > AR 38 > NER 824 > 31689
070	"	"	"	"	"	"	253 > 39 > BAR 39 > EBR (Pakistan) 39
071	"	"	"	"	"	"	254 > 40 > BAR 40 > EBR (Pakistan) 40
072	"	"	"	"	"	"	255 > 41 > BAR 41 > EBR (Pakistan) 41
073	"	"	"	"	"	"	256 > 42 > BAR 42 > EBR (Pakistan) 42
074	"	"	"	"	"	"	257 > 43 > BAR 43 > EBR (Pakistan) 43
075	"	"	"	"	"	"	258 > 44 > BAR 44 > EBR (Pakistan) 44
076	"	"	"	"	"	"	259 > 45 > BAR 45 > AR 45 > NER 825 > 31690
077	"	"	"	"	"	"	260 > 46 > BAR 46 > AR 46 > NER 826 > 31691
078	"	"	"	"	"	"	261 > 47 > BAR 47 > EBR (Pakistan) 47
079	"	"	"	"	"	"	262 > 48 > BAR 48 > AR 48 > NER 827 > 31692
080	"	"	"	"	"	"	263 > 49 > BAR 49 > EBR (Pakistan) 49
081	"	"	"	"	"	"	264 > 50 > BAR 50 > AR 50 > NER 828 > 31693
082	"	"	"	"	"	"	265 > 51 > BAR 51 > AR 51 > NER 829 > 31694
083	"	"	"	"	"	"	266 > 52 > BAR 52 > AR 52 > NER 830 > 31695

Works No.	Dispatch Date	Type	Cylinders	Driving Wheels	Gauge	Customer	Customer Name or Number
1084	1915	4-6-0	16½ x 22	4' 9"	Metre	Eastern Bengal State	267 > 53 > BAR 53 > AR 53 > NER 831 > 31696
1085	"	"	"	"	"	"	268 > 54 > BAR 54 > EBR (Pakistan) 54
1086	"	"	"	"	"	"	269 > 55 > BAR 55 > EBR (Pakistan) 55
1087	1915	2-8-2	16 x 18	2' 10	2' 6"	Bengal Nagpur, India	0076 > SER 613
1088	"	"	"	"	"	"	0077 > SER 614
1089	"	"	"	"	"	"	0078 > SER 615
1090	"	"	"	"	"	"	0079
1091	"	"	"	"	"	"	0080 > SER 616
1092	"	"	"	"	"	"	0081 > SER 617
1093	"	"	"	"	"	"	0082 > SER 618
1094	"	"	"	"	"	"	0083 > SER 619
1095	1915	4-8-0	16 x 22	3' 7"	Metre	Nizams Guaranteed State, India	Commandeered by War Office and shipped in March 1916 to Uganda 1095 > 1098 >200-203
1096	"	"	"	"	"	"	
1097	"	"	"	"	"	"	
1098	"	"	"	"	"	"	
1099 to 1105 were cancelled due to war conditions							
1106	1915	2-6-0T	18 x 26	4' 8½"	5' 6"	Bombay Port Trust	9 > Indian Iron & Steel Co.
1107	"	"	"	"	"	"	10
1108	"	"	"	"	"	"	11
1109	"	"	"	"	"	"	12
1110	"	"	"	"	"	"	13
1111	"	"	"	"	"	"	14
1112 to 1114 were cancelled due to war conditions							
1115 to 1119 were passed over to Beyer Peacock & Co for construction (4-4-2Ts for Gt. Northern of Ireland)							
1120	1916	2-8-0	23¼ x 25½	4' 8¾"	4' 8½"	French State	140.251
1121	"	"	"	"	"	"	140.252
1122	"	"	"	"	"	"	140.253
1123	"	"	"	"	"	"	140.254
1124	"	"	"	"	"	"	140.255
1125	"	"	"	"	"	"	140.256
1126	"	"	"	"	"	"	140.257
1127	"	"	"	"	"	"	140.258
1128	1917	"	"	"	"	"	140.259
1129	"	"	"	"	"	"	140.260
1130	"	"	"	"	"	"	140.261
1131	"	"	"	"	"	"	140.262
1132	"	"	"	"	"	"	140.263
1133	"	"	"	"	"	"	140.264
1134	"	"	"	"	"	"	140.265
1135	"	"	"	"	"	"	140.266
1136	"	"	"	"	"	"	140.267
1137	"	"	"	"	"	"	140.268
1138	"	"	"	"	"	"	140.269
1139	"	"	"	"	"	"	140.270
1140	1920	4-8-0	17 x 22	3' 7"	Metre	Nizams Guaranteed State, India	191
1141	"	"	"	"	"	"	192
1142	"	"	"	"	"	"	193
1143	"	"	"	"	"	"	194
1144	1917	0-4-0 Petrol	–	2' 8"	600cm	Ministry of Munitions	2001
1145	"	Electric	–	"	"	"	2002
1146	"	Tractors	–	"	"	"	2003
1147	"	"	–	"	"	"	2004
1148	"	"	–	"	"	"	2005
1149	"	"	–	"	"	"	2006
1150	"	"	–	"	"	"	2007
1151	"	"	–	"	"	"	2008
1152	"	"	–	"	"	"	2009
1153	"	"	–	"	"	"	2010
1154	"	"	–	"	"	"	2011
1155	"	"	–	"	"	"	2012
1156	"	"	–	"	"	"	2013
1157	"	"	–	"	"	"	2014
1158	"	"	–	"	"	"	2015
1159	"	"	–	"	"	"	2016
1160	"	"	–	"	"	"	2017
1161	"	"	–	"	"	"	2018
1162	"	"	–	"	"	"	2019
1163	"	"	–	"	"	"	2020
1164	"	"	–	"	"	"	2021
1165	"	"	–	"	"	"	2022
1166	"	"	–	"	"	"	2023
1167	"	"	–	"	"	"	2024

Works No.	Dispatch Date	Type	Cylinders	Driving Wheels	Gauge	Customer	Customer Name or Number
168	1917	Tractors	–	2' 8"	600 cm	Ministry of Munitions	2025
169	"	"	–	"	"	"	2026
170	"	"	–	"	"	"	2027
171	"	"	–	"	"	"	2028
172	"	"	–	"	"	"	2029
173	"	"	–	"	"	"	2030
174	"	"	–	"	"	"	2031
175	"	"	–	"	"	"	2032
176	"	"	–	"	"	"	2033
177	"	"	–	"	"	"	2034
178	"	"	–	"	"	"	2035
179	"	"	–	"	"	"	2036
180	"	"	–	"	"	"	2037
181	"	"	–	"	"	"	2038
182	"	"	–	"	"	"	2039
183	"	"	–	"	"	"	2040
184	"	"	–	"	"	"	2041
185	"	"	–	"	"	"	2042
186	"	"	–	"	"	"	2043
187	"	"	–	"	"	"	2044
188	"	"	–	"	"	"	2045
189	"	"	–	"	"	"	2046
190	"	"	–	"	"	"	2047
191	"	"	–	"	"	"	2048
192	"	"	–	"	"	"	2049
193	"	"	–	"	"	"	2050
194	"	"	–	"	"	"	2051
195	"	"	–	"	"	"	2052
196	"	"	–	"	"	"	2053
197	"	"	–	"	"	"	2054
198	"	"	–	"	"	"	2055
199	"	"	–	"	"	"	2056
200	"	"	–	"	"	"	2057
201	"	"	–	"	"	"	2058
202	"	"	–	"	"	"	2059
203	"	"	–	"	"	"	2060
204	"	"	–	"	"	"	2061
205	"	"	–	"	"	"	2062
206	"	"	–	"	"	"	2063
207	"	"	–	"	"	"	2064
208	"	"	–	"	"	"	2065
209	"	"	–	"	"	"	2066
210	"	"	–	"	"	"	2067
211	"	"	–	"	"	"	2068
212	"	"	–	"	"	"	2069
213	"	"	–	"	"	"	2070
214	"	"	–	"	"	"	2071
215	"	"	–	"	"	"	2072
216	"	"	–	"	"	"	2073
217	"	"	–	"	"	"	2074
218	"	"	–	"	"	"	2075
219	"	"	–	"	"	"	2076
220	"	"	–	"	"	"	2077
221	"	"	–	"	"	"	2078
222	"	"	–	"	"	"	2079
223	"	"	–	"	"	"	2080
224	"	"	–	"	"	"	2081
225	"	"	–	"	"	"	2082
226	"	"	–	"	"	"	2083
227	"	"	–	"	"	"	2084
228	"	"	–	"	"	"	2085
229	"	"	–	"	"	"	2086
230	"	"	–	"	"	"	2087
231	"	"	–	"	"	"	2088
232	"	"	–	"	"	"	2089
233	"	"	–	"	"	"	2090
234	"	"	–	"	"	"	2091
235	"	"	–	"	"	"	2092
236	"	"	–	"	"	"	2093
237	"	"	–	"	"	"	2094
238	"	"	–	"	"	"	2095
239	"	"	–	"	"	"	2096
240	"	"	–	"	"	"	2097
241	"	"	–	"	"	"	2098
242	"	"	–	"	"	"	2099

Works No.	Dispatch Date	Type	Cylinders	Driving Wheels	Gauge	Customer	Customer Name or Number
1243	1917	Tractors	–	2' 8"	600 cm	Ministry of Munitions	2100
1244	1917	2-8-0	21 x 26	4' 8"	SG	War Office ROD	1701 > LNER 6554
1245	"	"	"	"	"	"	1702 > China
1246	"	"	"	"	"	"	1703 > China
1247	"	"	"	"	"	"	1704 > GWR 3027
1248	"	"	"	"	"	"	1705 > China
1249	"	"	"	"	"	"	1706 > LMSR (Sold)
1250	"	"	"	"	"	"	1707 > LMSR (Sold)
1251	"	"	"	"	"	"	1708 > GWR 3032
1252	"	"	"	"	"	"	1709 > GWR 3047
1253	"	"	"	"	"	"	1710 > China
1254	"	"	"	"	"	"	1711 > China
1255	"	"	"	"	"	"	1712 > LNER 6555
1256	"	"	"	"	"	"	1713 > LNER 6556
1257	1918	"	"	"	"	"	1714 > LMSR (Scrap)
1258	"	"	"	"	"	"	1715 > LMSR (Sold)
1259	"	"	"	"	"	"	1716 > LNER 6557
1260	"	"	"	"	"	"	1717 > LNER 6536
1261	"	"	"	"	"	"	1718 > LNER 6377
1262	"	"	"	"	"	"	1719 > LNER 6537
1263	"	"	"	"	"	"	1720 > LMSR (Sold)
1264	"	"	"	"	"	"	1721 > LNER 6376
1265	"	"	"	"	"	"	1722 > LNER 6558
1266	"	"	"	"	"	"	1723 > LNER 6375
1267	"	"	"	"	"	"	1724 > LNER 6559
1268	1921	0-6-0 Crane	13 x 22	3' 0"	SG	Nasmyth Wilson & Co. Ltd.	JAMES NASMYTH > Cowpen Coal Co. 15 (0-6-0T)
1269	1919	0-6-2T	(18½ x 26)	5' 3"	SG	Taff Vale Railway	133 > GWR 367
1270	"	"	"	"	"	"	135 > GWR 370
1271	"	"	"	"	"	"	136 > GWR 371
1272	"	"	"	"	"	"	138 > GWR 372
1273	"	"	"	"	"	"	139 > GWR 373
1274	"	"	"	"	"	"	140 > GWR 374
1275	"	"	"	"	"	"	154 > GWR 377
1276	"	"	"	"	"	"	156 > GWR 378
1277	"	"	"	"	"	"	157 > GWR 379
1278	"	"	"	"	"	"	158 > GWR 380
1279	"	"	"	"	"	"	159 > GWR 381
1280	"	"	"	"	"	"	160 > GWR 382
1281	1919	2-8-0	21 x 26	4' 8"	SG	War Office ROD	1725 > GWR 3028
1282	"	"	"	"	"	"	1726 > GWR 3026
1283	"	"	"	"	"	"	1727 > LNER 6560
1284	"	"	"	"	"	"	1728 > LNER 6561
1285	"	"	"	"	"	"	1729 > LNER 6538
1286	"	"	"	"	"	"	1730 > GWR 3069
1287	"	"	"	"	"	"	1731 > GWR 3061
1288	"	"	"	"	"	"	1732 > GWR 3075
1289	1920	4-8-0	17 x 22	3' 7"	Metre	Nizams Guaranteed State, India	195 > AR 195 > NER 962 > 31885
1290	"	"	"	"	"	"	196
1291	"	"	"	"	"	"	197 > AR 197 > NER 963 > 31886
1292	"	"	"	"	"	"	198 > AR 198 > NER 964 > 31887
1293	"	"	"	"	"	"	199 > CR 31014
1294	1920	4-6-0	16 x 22	4' 0"	Metre	Rohilkund & Kumaon, India	81 > OTR 681 > NER 522 > 31776
1295	"	"	"	"	"	"	82 > OTR 682 > NER 523 > 31777
1296	"	"	"	"	"	"	83 > OTR 683 > NER 524 > 31778
1297	"	"	"	"	"	"	84 > OTR 684 > NER 525 > 31779
1298	"	"	"	"	"	"	85 > OTR 685 > NER 518 > 31772
1299	"	"	"	"	"	"	86 > OTR 686 > NER 519 > 31773
1300	"	"	"	"	"	"	87 > OTR 687 > NER 520 > 31774
1301	"	"	"	"	"	"	88 > OTR 688 > NER 521 > 31775
1302	1920	4-6-0	16 x 22	4' 0"	Metre	South Indian Railway	B70 > SR 31374
1303	"	"	"	"	"	"	B71 > SR 31375
1304	"	"	"	"	"	"	B72 > Iraq 176
1305	"	"	"	"	"	"	B73 > SR 31376
1306	"	"	"	"	"	"	B74
1307	"	"	"	"	"	"	B75 > Iraq 177
1308	"	"	"	"	"	"	B76 > SR 31377
1309	"	"	"	"	"	"	B77 > SR 31378
1310	"	"	"	"	"	"	B78 > SR 31379
1311	"	"	"	"	"	"	B81 > Iraq 178
1312	"	"	"	"	"	"	B82
1313	"	"	"	"	"	"	B83
1314	"	"	"	"	"	"	B84 > Iraq 179
1315	"	"	"	"	"	"	B85 > Iraq 180
1316	1921	"	"	"	"	"	B86

Works No.	Dispatch Date	Type	Cylinders	Driving Wheels	Gauge	Customer	Customer Name or Number
17	1921	4-6-0	16 x 22	4' 0"	Metre	South Indian Railway	B87
18	"	"	"	"	"	"	B88 > Iraq 181
19	"	"	"	"	"	"	B89 > Iraq 182
20	"	"	"	"	"	"	B90 > Iraq 183
21	"	"	"	"	"	"	B91 > SR 31381
22	1921	4-6-0	16 x 22	4' 0"	Metre	Assam Bengal	146 > BAR 143 > Iraq 167
23	"	"	"	"	"	"	147 > BAR 144 > AR 144 > NER 586 > 31846
24	"	"	"	"	"	"	148 > BAR 145
25	"	"	"	"	"	"	149 > BAR 146 > AR 146 > NER 587 > 31847
26	"	"	"	"	"	"	150 > BAR 147 > AR 147 > NER 588 > 31848
27	"	"	"	"	"	"	151 > BAR 148 > AR 148 > NER 589 > 31849
28	"	"	"	"	"	"	152 > BAR 149 > AR 149 > NER 590 > 31850
29	"	"	"	"	"	"	153 > BAR 150 > AR 150 > NER 591 > 31851
30	"	"	"	"	"	"	154 > BAR 151 > AR 151 > NER 592 > 31852
31	"	"	"	"	"	"	155 > BAR 152 > EBR (Pakistan) 152
32	"	"	"	"	"	"	156 > BAR 153 > EBR (Pakistan) 153
33	1921	4-6-0	16 x 22	4' 0"	Metre	Burma Railway	396 > RSR (Thailand) 198
34	"	"	"	"	"	"	397
35	"	"	"	"	"	"	398
36	"	"	"	"	"	"	399
37	"	"	"	"	"	"	400
38	"	"	"	"	"	"	401
39	"	"	"	"	"	"	402
40	"	"	"	"	"	"	403
41	"	"	"	"	"	"	404
42	"	"	"	"	"	"	405
43	"	"	"	"	"	"	406
44	"	"	"	"	"	"	407
45	"	"	"	"	"	"	408
46	"	"	"	"	"	"	409
47	"	"	"	"	"	"	410
48	"	"	"	"	"	"	411
49	"	"	"	"	"	"	412
50	1921	4-8-0	17 x 22	3' 7"	Metre	Uganda Railway	119
51	"	"	"	"	"	"	120
52	1921	4-6-0	16 x 22	4' 0"	Metre	Assam Bengal	154 > BAR 154 > EBR (Pakistan) 154
53	1921	4-6-0	16 x 22	4' 0"	Metre	Gold Coast	40
54	"	"	"	"	"	"	41
55	"	"	"	"	"	"	42
56	"	"	"	"	"	"	43
57	1922	2-10-2T	23½ x 26	4' 3"	5' 6"	Bombay Port Trust	25
58	"	"	"	"	"	"	26
59	1921	2-6-0T	18 x 26	4' 8½"	"	"	15
60	"	"	"	"	"	"	16
61	"	"	"	"	"	"	17
62	"	"	"	"	"	"	18
63	"	"	"	"	"	"	19
64	"	"	"	"	"	"	20
65	"	"	"	"	"	"	21
66	"	"	"	"	"	"	22
67	"	"	"	"	"	"	23
68	"	"	"	"	"	"	24
69	1922	4-6-0	16 x 22	4' 0"	Metre	South Indian Railway	B 96 > Iraq 184
70	"	"	"	"	"	"	B 97 > Iraq 185
71	1922	2-8-2	16 x 18	2' 10"	2' 6"	Bengal Nagpur, India	0096 > SER 632
72	"	"	"	"	"	"	0097 > SER 633
73	"	"	"	"	"	"	0098 > SER 634
74	"	"	"	"	"	"	0099 > SER 635
75	"	"	"	"	"	"	0100 > SER 636
76	1922	4-6-0	16 x 22	4' 0"	Metre	Aden Railway	No. 1 > EBR 325 > BAR 325 > EBR (Pakistan) 325
77	1922	2-8-2	20½ x 24	3' 9"	3' 6"	Gold Coast, Takoradi Harbour Works	11 AHANTA > Gold Coast Govt. 201
78	"	"	"	"	"	"	12 FANTI > Gold Coast Govt. 202
79	"	"	"	"	"	"	13 HAUSA > Gold Coast Govt. 203
80	"	"	"	"	"	"	14 TWI > Gold Coast Govt. 204
81	"	"	"	"	"	"	15 GA > Gold Coast Govt. 213
82	"	"	"	"	"	"	16 EPHE > Gold Coast Govt. 214
83	1922	4-8-0	18 x 23	3' 6¾"	3' 6"	Nigerian Railway	211
84	"	"	"	"	"	"	212
85	"	"	"	"	"	"	213
86	"	"	"	"	"	"	214
87	"	"	"	"	"	"	215
88	"	"	"	"	"	"	216
89	1922	4-6-0	16½ x 22	4' 9"	Metre	Bengal & North Western	360 > OTR 360 > NER 743 > 31573
90	"	"	"	"	"	"	361 > OTR 361 > NER 744 > 31574

Works No.	Dispatch Date	Type	Cylinders	Driving Wheels	Gauge	Customer	Customer Name or Number
1391	1922	4-6-0	16½ x 22	4' 9"	Metre	Bengal & North Western	362 > OTR 362 > NER 745 > 31575
1392	"	"	"	"	"	"	363 > OTR 363 > NER 746 > 31576
1393	1923	2-8-2	20½ x 24	3' 9"	3' 6"	Gold Coast, Takoradi Harbour Works	> Gold Coast 171 > 205
1394	"	"	"	"	"	"	> Gold Coast 172 > 206
1395	1923	4-6-0	16½ x 22	4' 9"	Metre	Bengal & North Western	364 > OTR 364 > NER 747 > 31577
1396	"	"	"	"	"	"	365 > OTR 365 > NER 748 > 31578
1397	"	"	"	"	"	"	366 > OTR 366 > NER 749 > 31579
1398	"	"	"	"	"	"	367 > OTR 367 > NER 750 > 31580
1399	"	"	"	"	"	"	368 > OTR 368 > NER 751 > 31581
1400	"	"	"	"	"	"	369 > OTR 369 > NER 752 > 31582
1401	1923	4-6-4T	16½ x 22	4' 9"	Metre	South Indian Railway	MT1 > SR 37351
1402	"	"	"	"	"	"	MT2 > SR 37352
1403	"	"	"	"	"	"	MT3 > SR 37353
1404	"	"	"	"	"	"	MT4 > SR 37354
1405	"	"	"	"	"	"	MT5 > SR 37355
1406	"	"	"	"	"	"	MT6 > SR 37356
1407	"	"	"	"	"	"	MT7 > SR 37357
1408	"	"	"	"	"	"	MT8 > SR 37358
1409	1923	4-8-0	17 x 22	3' 7"	Metre	Nizams Guaranteed State, India	200 > CR 31015
1410	"	"	"	"	"	"	201 > CR 31016
1411	"	"	"	"	"	"	202 > CR 31017
1412	1924	2-8-2	18¼ x 23½	3' 7½"	Metre	Siam State	311
1413	"	"	"	"	"	"	312
1414	1924	2-8-2	20½ x 24	3' 9"	3' 6"	Gold Coast	207
1415	"	"	"	"	"	"	208
1416	"	"	"	"	"	"	209
1417	"	"	"	"	"	"	210
1418	1924	0-6-0T	11 x 16	2' 9"	3' 6"	Castlecliff, NZ	
1419	1924	0-8-0T	17 x 23	3' 6"	SG	Astley & Tyldesley Colliery	EMANUEL CLEGG
1420	1924	4-8-0	18 x 23	4' 0"	3' 6"	Nigerian Railway	606
1421	"	"	"	"	"	"	607 PRINCE OF WALES
1422	"	"	"	"	"	"	608
1423	1924	4-4-2T	(18 x 24)	5' 9"	5' 3"	Gt. Northern of Ireland	21
1424	"	"	"	"	"	"	30
1425	"	"	"	"	"	"	115
1426	"	"	"	"	"	"	116
1427	"	"	"	"	"	"	139
1428	"	0-6-0	(19 x 26)	5' 1"	"	"	15
1429	"	"	"	"	"	"	16
1430	"	"	"	"	"	"	17
1431	"	"	"	"	"	"	18
1432	"	"	"	"	"	"	19
1433	1924	2-8-2	20½ x 24	3' 9"	3' 6"	Gold Coast	211
1434	"	"	"	"	"	"	212
1435	"	4-4-2T	(18 x 24)	5' 9"	5' 3"	Gt. Northern of Ireland	142
1436	"	"	"	"	"	"	143
1437	"	"	"	"	"	"	144
1438	"	"	"	"	"	"	147
1439	"	"	"	"	"	"	148
1440	"	4-6-0	14½ x 20	4' 0"	Metre	Bikaner, India	26 > NR 26 > 31421
1441	"	"	"	"	"	"	27 > NR 27 > 31422
1442	"	"	"	"	"	"	28 > NR 28 > 31423
1443	"	"	"	"	"	"	29 > NR 29 > 31424
1444	"	"	"	"	"	"	30 > NR 30 > 31425
1445	"	"	"	"	"	"	31 > NR 31 > 31426
1446	"	"	"	"	"	"	32 > NR 32 > 31427
1447	"	"	"	"	"	"	33 > NR 33 > 31428
1448	1925	4-4-2T	19 x 26	6' 6"	4' 8½"	London Midland & Scottish	2120 > 41938
1449	"	"	"	"	"	"	2121 > 41939
1450	"	"	"	"	"	"	2122 > 41940
1451	"	"	"	"	"	"	2123 > 41941
1452	"	"	"	"	"	"	2124 > 41942
1453	"	0-4-4T	18¼ x 26	5' 9"	"	"	15260 > 55260
1454	"	"	"	"	"	"	15261 > 55261
1455	"	"	"	"	"	"	15262 > 55262
1456	"	"	"	"	"	"	15263 > 55263
1457	"	"	"	"	"	"	15264 > 55264
1458	"	"	"	"	"	"	15265 > 55265
1459	"	"	"	"	"	"	15266 > 55266
1460	"	"	"	"	"	"	15267 > 55267
1461	"	"	"	"	"	"	15268 > 55268
1462	"	"	"	"	"	"	15269 > 55269
1463	1925	2-6-2T	15 x 22	3' 7"	Metre	Jodhpur, India	01 > NR 1 > 32040
1464	"	"	"	"	"	"	02 > NR 2 > 32041
1465	"	2-8-2	17½ x 22	3' 8"	"	"	090 > NR 177 > 32034

Works No.	Dispatch Date	Type	Cylinders	Driving Wheels	Gauge	Customer	Customer Name or Number
1466	1925	2-8-2	17½ x 22	3' 8"	Metre	Jodhpur, India	091 > NR 178 > 32035
1467	"	"	"	"	"	"	092 > NR 179 > 32036
1468	"	"	"	"	"	"	093 > NR 180 > 32037
1469	"	"	"	"	"	"	094 > NR 181 > 32038
1470	"	"	"	"	"	"	095 > NR 182 > 32039
1471	1926	4-6-2	18 x 26	5' 0"	3' 6"	Nigerian Railway	405 ALAKE OF ABEOKUTA
1472	"	"	"	"	"	"	406 AWAJALE OF IJEBU-ODE
1473	"	"	"	"	"	"	407 ALAFIN OF OYO
1474	"	"	"	"	"	"	408 ONI OF IFE
1475	"	"	"	"	"	"	409 OBA OF BENIN
1476	"	"	"	"	"	"	410 MARY SLESSOR
1477	1926	2-6-2T	15 x 22	3' 7"	Metre	Burma Railway	58
1478	"	"	"	"	"	"	59
1479	"	"	"	"	"	"	60
1480	"	"	"	"	"	"	61
1481	"	"	"	"	"	"	62
1482	1926	2-8-2	15½ x 18	2' 10"	2' 6"	Barsi Light, India	19 > CR 712
1483	"	"	"	"	"	"	20 > CR 713
1484	"	"	"	"	"	"	21 > CR 714
1485	"	"	"	"	"	"	22 > CR 715
1486	"	"	"	"	"	"	23 > CR 716
1487	1926	2-8-2	16 x 18	2' 10"	2' 6"	Gt. Indian Peninsula, Central Provinces	13 > CR 770
1488	"	"	"	"	"	"	14 > CR 771
1489	1926	4-6-0	15 x 22	4' 0"	5' 6"	Ceylon Govt.	229
1490	"	"	"	"	"	"	230
1491	"	"	"	"	"	"	231
1492	1927	2-6-2T	15 x 22	3' 7"	Metre	Jodhpur, India	03 > NR 3 > 32042
1493	1927	4-6-4T	18 x 22	4' 6"	3' 6"	Nigerian Railway	451
1494	"	"	"	"	"	"	452
1495	"	"	"	"	"	"	453
1496	"	"	"	"	"	"	454
1497	1927	0-6-0	(19½ x 26)	4' 7"	5' 6"	South Indian Railway	K58 > SR 37059
1498	"	"	"	"	"	"	K59 > SR 37060
1499	"	"	"	"	"	"	K60 > SR 37061
1500	"	"	"	"	"	"	K61 > SR 37062
1501	"	"	"	"	"	"	K62 > SR 37063
1502	"	"	"	"	"	"	K63 > SR 37064
1503	"	"	"	"	"	"	K64 > SR 37065
1504	"	"	"	"	"	"	K65 > SR 37066
1505	1927	2-8-2	17 x 24	4' 0"	Metre	Bombay, Baroda & Central India	283 > WR 30194
1506	"	"	"	"	"	"	324 > WR 30195
1507	1927	2-8-2	17 x 24	4' 0"	Metre	Madras & Southern Mahratta, India	430 > SR 30254
1508	"	"	"	"	"	"	431 > SR 30255
1509	1927	2-8-2	17 x 24	4' 0"	Metre	Burma Railway	427
1510	"	"	"	"	"	"	428
1511	"	"	"	"	"	"	429
1512	"	"	"	"	"	"	430
1513	"	"	"	"	"	"	431
1514	"	"	"	"	"	"	432
1515	"	"	"	"	"	"	433
1516	1927	4-6-2	16 x 24	4' 9"	Metre	Eastern Bengal Railway	401 > BAR 401 > AR 401 > NER 1030 > 30108
1517	"	"	"	"	"	"	402 > BAR 402 > AR 402 > NER 1031 > 30109
1518	1927	4-6-2	16 x 24	4' 9"	Metre	Bengal & North Western	370 > OTR 370 > NER 1001 > 30079
1519	"	"	"	"	"	"	371 > OTR 371 > NER 1002 > 30080
1520	1928	4-6-2	17½ x 24	4' 9"	Metre	Madras & Southern Mahratta, India	414 > 550 > SR 30139
1521	"	"	"	"	"	"	415 > 551 > SR 30140
1522	"	"	"	"	"	"	416 > 552 > SR 30141
1523	1928	4-6-2	17½ x 24	4' 9"	Metre	Bombay, Baroda & Central India	328 > MSMR 563 > SR 30152
1524	"	"	"	"	"	"	347 > MSMR 564 > SR 30153
1525	1927	2-8-2	15½ x 18	2' 10"	2' 6"	Barsi Light, India	29 > CR 717
1526	"	"	"	"	"	"	30 > CR 718
1527	1928	4-6-0	16½ x 22	4' 9"	Metre	Bengal & North Western	372 > OTR 372 > NER 793 > 31622
1528	"	"	"	"	"	"	373 > OTR 373 > NER 794 > 31623
1529	"	"	"	"	"	"	374 > OTR 374 > NER 795 > 31624
1530	"	"	"	"	"	"	375 > OTR 375 > NER 796 > 31625
1531	"	2-8-2	16 x 18	2' 10"	2' 6"	India North Western	190 > 221 > NR 93
1532	"	"	"	"	"	"	191 > 222 > NR 94
1533	"	4-6-2	18 x 26	5' 0"	3' 6"	Nigerian Railway	411 EMIR OF ILORIN
1534	"	"	"	"	"	"	412 EMIR OF KAIAMA
1535	"	"	"	"	"	"	413 RICHARD LANDER
1536	"	"	"	"	"	"	414 JEAN MARIE COQUARD
1537	"	4-8-0	17 x 22	3' 7"	Metre	Bengal Dooars	18 > EBR 118 > BAR 140 > AR 140 > NER 943 > 31802

Works No.	Dispatch Date	Type	Cylinders	Driving Wheels	Gauge	Customer	Customer Name or Number
1538	1928	4-8-0	17 x 22	3' 7"	Metre	Bengal Dooars	19 > EBR 119 > BAR 141 > AR 141 > NER 944 > 31803
1539	"	4-6-4	15 x 18	3' 6"	2' 6"	Barsi Light, India	31 > CR 728
1540	"	"	"	"	"	"	32 > CR 729
1541	"	"	"	"	"	"	33 > CR 730
1542	"	"	"	"	"	"	34 > CR 731
1543	"	"	"	"	"	"	35 > CR 732
1544	1929	4-6-2	16 x 24	4' 9"	Metre	Indian State, Eastern Bengal	403 > BAR 403 > AR 403 > 1032 > 30110
1545	"	"	"	"	"	"	404 > BAR 404 > AR 404 > 1033 > 30111
1546	"	"	"	"	"	"	405 > BAR 405 > AR 405 > 1034 > 30112
1547	"	"	"	"	"	"	406 > BAR 406 > EBR (Pakistan) 406
1548	"	"	"	"	"	"	407 > BAR 407 > EBR (Pakistan) 407
1549	"	"	"	"	"	"	408 > BAR 408 > EBR (Pakistan) 408
1550	"	"	"	"	"	"	409 > ABR 251 > BAR 409 > AR 409 > 1035 > 30113
1551	"	"	"	"	"	"	410 > ABR 252 > BAR 410 > AR 410 > 1036 > 30114
1552	"	"	"	"	"	"	411 > ABR 253 > BAR 411 > EBR (Pakistan) 411
1553	"	"	"	"	"	"	412 > ABR 254 > BAR 412 > AR 412 > 1037 > 30115
1554	"	"	"	"	"	"	413 > ABR 255 > BAR 413 > AR 413 > 1038 > 30116
1555	"	"	"	"	"	"	414 > BAR 414 > EBR (Pakistan) 414
1556	"	"	"	"	"	"	415 > BAR 415 > AR 415 > 1039 > 30117
1557	1929	"	"	"	Metre	South Indian Railway	YB 7 > SR 30050
1558	"	"	"	"	"	"	YB 8 > SR 30051
1559	"	"	"	"	"	"	YB 9 > SR 30052
1560	"	"	"	"	"	"	YB 10 > SR 30053
1561	"	"	"	"	"	"	YB 11 > SR 30054
1562	1929	2-8-2	17 x 24	4' 0"	Metre	Gondal, India	No 1 > Saurashtra 1 > WR 157 > 30191
1563	1929	2-6-2	12 x 18	2' 10"	2' 6"	Bengal Nagpur Raipur Dhamtari, India	07 > SER 687
1564	"	"	"	"	"	"	08 > SER 688
1565	"	"	"	"	"	"	09 > SER 689
1566	"	"	"	"	"	"	010 > SER 690
1567	1929	4-6-4T	14½ x 22	4' 6"	Metre	Federated Malay States	18 > MR 401.01
1568	"	"	"	"	"	"	19 > MR 401.02
1569	"	"	"	"	"	"	20 > MR 401.03
1570	"	"	"	"	"	"	21 > MR 401.04
1571	"	"	"	"	"	"	22 > MR 401.05
1572	1929	4-6-2	16 x 24	4' 9"	Metre	Nizams Guaranteed State, India	175 > CR 30002
1573	"	"	"	"	"	"	176 > CR 30003
1574	1929	2-8-2	15½ x 18	2' 10"	2' 6"	Barsi Light, India	36 > CR 719
1575	"	"	"	"	"	"	37 > CR 720
1576	"	"	"	"	"	"	38 > CR 721
1577	1930	4-6-0	15 x 22	4' 0"	Metre	Mysore State	75 > 66 > 56 > SR 31227
1578	"	"	"	"	"	"	76 > 67 > 57 > SR 31228
1579	"	"	"	"	"	"	77 > 68 > 58 > SR 31229
1580	1930	4-8-0	18 x 22	3' 7"	Metre	Kenya & Uganda	218 > EAR & H 2457
1581	"	"	"	"	"	"	219 > EAR & H 2458
1582	"	"	"	"	"	"	220 > EAR & H 2459
1583	"	"	"	"	"	"	221 > EAR & H 2460
1584	"	"	"	"	"	"	222 > EAR & H 2461
1585	"	"	"	"	"	"	223 > EAR & H 2462
1586	1930	4-6-4	15 x 18	3' 6"	2' 6"	Barsi Light, India	4 > CR 725
1587	"	"	"	"	"	"	5 > CR 726
1588	1930	4-8-0	16 x 22	3' 7"	Metre	Tanganyika Railway	29 > 213 > EAR & H 2214
1589	"	"	"	"	"	"	30 > 214 > EAR & H 2215
1590	"	"	"	"	"	"	31 > 215 > EAR & H 2216
1591	"	"	"	"	"	"	32 > 216 > EAR & H 2217
1592	1931	0-8-0T	15¼ x 20	3' 4"	SG	Jamaica Govt.	6
1593	"	"	"	"	"	"	8
1594	1932	2-8-2	20 x 28	4' 6"	"	Chinese Govt. Tientsin Pukow	291
1595	"	"	"	"	"	"	292
1596	"	"	"	"	"	"	293
1597	"	"	"	"	"	"	294
1598	"	"	"	"	"	"	295
1599	"	"	"	"	"	"	296
1600	"	"	"	"	"	"	297
1601	"	"	"	"	"	"	298
1602	1933	2-8-0	15 x 20	3' 0"	2' 5½"	Egyptian State, Western Oasis	1 > 2001
1603	"	"	"	"	"	"	2 > 2002
1604	1934	4-6-0	15 x 22	4' 0"	Metre	Bhavnagar State	41 > Saurashtra 112 > WR 31097
1605	"	"	"	"	"	"	42 > Saurashtra 113 > WR 31098
1606	1934	4-8-2T	17½ x 24	3' 10"	SG	Jamaica Govt.	12

Works No.	Dispatch Date	Type	Cylinders	Driving Wheels	Gauge	Customer	Customer Name or Number
1607	1934	0-6-0T	17½ x 24	4' 0 "	SG	Palestine Railway	40
1608	"	"	"	"	"	"	41
1609	1935	"	"	"	"	"	42
1610	1935	4-6-2	16 x 24	4' 9"	Metre	Bengal & North Western, India	426 > OTR 426 > NER 1003 > 30081
1611	"	"	"	"	"	"	427 > OTR 427 > NER 1004 > 30082
1612	"	"	"	"	"	"	428 > OTR 428 > NER 1005 > 30083
1613	"	"	"	"	"	"	429 > OTR 429 > NER 1006 > 30084
1614	"	"	"	"	"	"	430 > OTR 430 > NER 1007 > 30085
1615	"	"	"	"	"	"	431 > OTR 431 > NER 1008 > 30086
1616	"	"	"	"	"	"	432 > OTR 432 > NER 1009 > 30087
1617	"	"	"	"	"	"	433 > OTR 433 > NER 1010 > 30088
1618	1935	2-8-2	21 x 26	4' 6"	SG	Kiao Tsi, China	
1619	"	"	"	"	"	"	
1620	"	"	"	"	"	"	
1621	"	"	"	"	"	"	
1622	1936	4-8-0	19 x 26	3' 10"	SG	Jamaica Govt.	30
1623	1936	0-6-0T	17½ x 24	4' 0"	SG	Palestine Railway	43
1624	"	"	"	"	"	"	44
1625	"	"	"	"	"	"	45
1626	"	"	"	"	"	"	46
1627	1936	4-8-2	18 x 24	4' 0"	3' 6"	Gold Coast Govt.	241
1628	"	"	"	"	"	"	242
1629	1936	0-6-0T	17½ x 24	4' 0"	SG	Palestine Railway	47
1630	"	"	"	"	"	"	48
1631	1936	4-6-0	14½ x 22	4' 0"	Metre	Junagad State	22 > Saurashtra 95 > WR 31170
1632	"	"	"	"	"	"	23 > Saurashtra 96 > WR 31171
1633	"	"	"	"	"	"	24 > Saurashtra 97 > WR 31172
1634	1936	4-8-2	18 x 24	4' 0"	3' 6"	Gold Coast Govt.	243
1635	"	"	"	"	"	"	244
1636	"	"	"	"	"	"	245
1637	1936	4-6-0	15 x 22	4' 0"	Metre	Bhavnagar State	43 > Saurashtra 114 > WR 31099
1638	"	"	"	"	"	"	44 > Saurashtra 115 > WR 31100
1639	1937	4-6-2	16 x 24	4' 9"	Metre	Bengal & North Western	434 > OTR 434 > NER 1011 > 30089
1640	"	"	"	"	"	"	435 > OTR 435 > NER 1012 > 30090
1641	"	"	"	"	"	"	436 > OTR 436 > NER 1013 > 30091
1642	"	"	"	"	"	"	437 > OTR 437 > NER 1014 > 30092
1643	"	2-6-2T	15 x 22	3' 7"	"	"	438 > OTR 438 > NER 142 > 32070
1644	"	"	"	"	"	"	439 > OTR 439 > NER 143 > 32071
1645	"	"	"	"	"	"	440 > OTR 440 > NER 144 > 32072
1646	"	"	"	"	"	"	441 > OTR 441 > NER 145 > 32073
1647	"	"	"	"	"	"	442 > OTR 442 > NER 146 > 32074
1648	"	"	"	"	"	"	443 > OTR 443 > NER 147 > 32075
1649	1938	2-6-4T	14 x 20	4' 0"	Metre	South Indian Railway	ST1 > SR 37366
1650	"	"	"	"	"	"	ST2 > SR 37367
1651	1938	0-6-0T	17½ x 24	4' 0"	SG	Palestine Railway	49
1652	"	"	"	"	"	"	50

Other local titles published by Tempus

The Willing Servant: A History of the Steam Locomotive
DAVID ROSS

Taking us through the last two hundred years, David Ross tells not just the story of the steam engine but also of its effects on mankind. From small beginnings, the railway locomotive was responsible for the speed of industrialisation in many countries, for commuting, for tourism, for industrial progress in all fields and for making the people of the world a transient workforce. Without it, the world would be a different place.
0 7524 2986 8

It's Quicker By Rail! The History of LNER Advertising
ALLAN MIDDLETON

The greatest proponents of publicity and advertising in the Art Deco period were the railway companies. Working with the finest of poster artists from Terence Cuneo to Frank Newbold and Frank Mason, the story of the LNER publicity department is an important addition to art and design history.
0 7524 2765 2

Manchester's Airport Ringway Remembered
BARRY ABRAHAM

The beginnings of Manchester Airport are found in the Alexandra Park Aerodrome and Wythenshawe, expanding to Barton Moss in 1930. The airport moved again in 1938 to its present site at Ringway. In the Second World War the site was taken up as a military base and was the home of the Parachute Training School. Air traffic boomed again in the 1970s and has been expanding ever since. This illustrated volume looks back over the history of the airport.
0 7524 2109 3

Central Manchester
PETER STEWART

This fascinating collection of over 200 old photographs, taken from postcards and other photographic archive sources, shows Manchester as it was not so very long ago and honours those who lived here and helped to make it the place it is today. This book includes a look at the changes that Manchester experienced in the first half of this century, the effects of the blitz and the post-war reconstruction.
0 7524 0322 2

If you are interested in purchasing other books published by Tempus, or in case you have difficulty finding any Tempus books in your local bookshop, you can also place orders directly through our website

www.tempus-publishing.com